***CrossCurrents*** (ISSN 0011-1953; online ISSN 1939-3881) connects the wisdom of the heart with the life of the mind and the experiences of the body. The journal is operated through its parent organization, the Association for Public Religion and Intellectual Life (APRIL), an interreligious network of academics, activists, artists, and community leaders seeking to engage the many ways religion meets the public. Contributions to the journal exist at the nexus of religion, education, the arts, and social justice. The journal is published quarterly on behalf of the Association for Public Religion and Intellectual Life by the University of North Carolina Press.

The Association for Public Religion and Intellectual Life (formerly ARIL) is a global network of leaders, scholars, and social change agents who explore religious life, engage in intellectual inquiry, and lead ethical action in the world today. Their primary objective, especially through annual summer colloquia and *CrossCurrents*, is to bring together leading voices of our time to advocate for justice and to examine global spiritual and interreligious currents in both historical and contemporary perspectives.

A membership to APRIL includes access to *CrossCurrents* starting with Volume 58, 2008, though our partners at Project MUSE, monthly newsletters, early access to summer colloquium themes, a 40% on UNC Press books, and more. For more information, including membership and subscription rates, visit www.aprilonline.org.

This reissue of *CrossCurrents* was one of four issues published in 2008 as part of Volume 58. For a current masthead visit www.aprilonline.org.

© 2008 Association for Public Religion and Intellectual Life. All rights reserved.

ISBN 978-1-4696-6686-0 (Print)

# CROSSCURRENTS
VOLUME 58, NO 4 ISSN 0011-1953

## EDITORIAL

**518**
Victor A. Kramer & Glenn Crider

## ARTICLES

**522**
"*The Surest Home Is Pointless*": A Pathless Path through Merton's Poetic Corpus
**Patrick F. O'Connell**

**545**
"*Love for the Paradise Mystery*" — Thomas Merton: Contemplative Ecologist
**Kathleen Deignan**

**570**
Thomas Merton's Re-Visioning the New World at Intercultural Borders
**Malgorzata Poks**

**592**
Thomas Merton's Contemplation: Rarefied Emblem of Being Human and Living in Mystery
**Glenn Crider**

**608**
Excerpts from the International Thomas Merton Society General Meeting (2005) and the American Benedictine Academy Convention (2008)
**John Eudes Bamberger & Sidney H. Griffith**

**613**
What to Listen for: Merton as Teacher — A Note
**Victor A. Kramer & Glenn Crider**

# BOOK

**616**
*Thomas Merton, Initiation into the Monastic Tradition, Vols. 1–3*
Mark DelCogliano

**621**
**Notes on Contributors**

On the Cover: Drawing by Thomas Merton. Used with permission of the Merton Legacy Trust and the Thomas Merton Center at Bellarmine University.

# EDITORIAL

## THOMAS MERTON GLOBAL PROPHET

Merton, grounded in the Christian monastic "School of Charity," stands as a prophet for humankind's future. On August 6, 1960 he wrote: "A prophet is one who cuts through great tangled webs of lies." His intense, compassionate vision, akin to Teilhard de Chardin's, invites all persons to embrace creation by employing a magnifying glass of compassion to ignite the ever-present rays of God's mercy. Then comes the living dance, what he calls the "general dance" in *New Seeds of Contemplation*. His vision includes ecumenical Christianity and sees beyond to affirm authenticity as manifested through art, culture, liturgies, and societal needs in the most inclusive religious and cultural senses. This issue of *CrossCurrents* commemorates forty years of Merton's earthly absence and paradoxically his increasing worldwide presence. It brings together insights about his power, which flows from obedience as a contemporary Christian monk choosing to live faithfully as a Cistercian within the unlikely culture of mid-twentieth century America. Merton lived almost fifty-four years and was a member of the community of the Abbey of Gethsemani in Kentucky from December 10, 1941 to December 10, 1968.

We are only now beginning to understand his amazing legacy. Sometimes I think of him as a Walt Whitman *and* a St. Augustine, or as an Emily Dickenson *and* a Thomas Aquinas. He was a towering intellectual, yet like Herman Melville's Ishmael, a mystical observer. He pondered the globe—its good and evil. His tale is multivalent. What is most significant is that through his writing the whole world became one community.

Merton's gift of renewal, a legacy rooted in the Desert Fathers and St. Benedict, is clearly needed for the future of all humankind. His contemplative vision is both very simple and simultaneously extraordinary. Buried by vows in the quiet of the knobs of Kentucky, he rose as spokesman for *all*. He saw the whole world in his vision as did Jesus, Benedict, and Gerard Manley Hopkins (his proposed Ph.D. topic at Columbia). Earlier his M.A. thesis was written on William Blake, done in the framework of neo-Thomism. Jacques Maritain's *Art and Scholasticism* informed Merton to think in big patterns even then. Finally, Merton's gift allowed him to stand back *for* the whole planet.

That is also what we are trying to do here with this special double-issue celebrating Merton. With this issue and the next, our intent is to help readers see Merton as one of the most important—indeed prophetic figures—in recent Western culture. He stands as a gift for all seekers in the twenty-first century. As a prophet, he cuts away confusion.

We have never before had a witness like Merton. Awake to all creation; alert to the horrors of the twentieth-century and all of the neo-colonial errors of 500 years, he sings the glory of God (yet not only as a Roman Catholic God) for a world which had become both post-Christian and, even more so, post-humane. His mature poetic-prose gathering, *Raids on the Unspeakable* (1966), is an intense collection of essays and meditations which allows us to see "the outrageousness of our cultural assumptions." Maybe more importantly, as reflected in the pieces collected here, we can see Merton found many excellent ways to affirm our world and our contemporary needs.

We hope these essays, testimonies, analyses, and book review allow readers to know Merton a bit better and to come closer to implementing his vision. He had a wonderfully expansive and loving vision: we know no other prophet who as cloistered monk so loved the world, and who so loved humanity as to write literally thousands of letters and hundreds of poems and scores of lectures and books to remind us of the "inner experience" which we are desperately in our Promethean madness so bent on running away from.

Brief excerpts included here are from two meetings where Merton was the focus.[1] These analysts also refer to him as Prophet. What is interesting is that these commentators approach him so utterly differently. In each instance, he is appreciated as someone whose radical intuition allows him to provide insight into and for our contemporary culture's needs. John Eudes Bamberger's view is filtered through personal friendship with Merton and allows us to see Merton's vision of monastic renewal growing out of a recovery of fundamental Cistercian traditions. Sidney Griffith has a totally different approach which allows us to understand Merton's complex interreligious dialogue (with many different religions) as rooted in personal encounter. For an overview of the thrust of the seven major essays, my co-editor's comments follow.

–Victor A. Kramer

**Note**

1. For information about the meetings from which these excerpts are derived consult websites for the American Benedictine Academy and for the International Thomas Merton Society at http://www.osb.org/aba/ and http://www.mertoncenter.org/ITMS/.

# COMMENTARY

Merton's radical mystical insight, a complete trust in "hidden wholeness," reveals an intuition, knowledge, and affirmation of God through embrace of contemplative wisdom. This fundamental insight became Merton's core poem, a unifying sustained prayer and a celebration of the assurance of God's presence. Such unifying certainty reminds us to make ourselves ready—living the mystery of our share in Divinity. Merton urges us to remain open to all persons and to the cosmos. Such Catholicism conjoined with kenotic trust, as taken seriously in the essays here, is revolutionary. Church and society, in their protectiveness, cannot yet accept such transformative teaching.

These essays offer insight into the multifaceted life and work of Thomas Merton. O'Connell's incisive classification and analytical scalpel allow readers of Merton's poetry to see how, like an Old Testament prophet, Merton saw, focused, and spoke. Deignan invites us into both the radiant world of a sometimes forgotten paradise and the significance of prophecy as a critique of humanity's ongoing need to "recover" paradise within our world. Poks demonstrates the expansive interconnected and vibrant living vision Merton cultivated for all the Americas. In my essay on Merton and contemplation, I suggest he intuits, embraces, and lives the mystery of what many try to "explain" yet, ironically, overlook. In the next issue, King shows us how readers unfamiliar with or distanced from the Benedictine/Cistercian tradition hunger for the "true education" of Merton's inclusive understanding of life. Farge, with great love of Merton and Catholicism, and Paramahansa Yogananda and Eastern religions, opens doors to East-West dialogue showing interconnectedness, which unlocks long-held prejudices and deepens our sense of "religion." Wu, from perspectives of his father (who worked with Merton) and culture, sees ecumenism as love and Merton as ecumenism's indispensable model.

—*Glenn Crider*

# "THE SUREST HOME IS POINTLESS"
## A Pathless Path through Merton's Poetic Corpus

Patrick F. O'Connell

Finding one's way through the 1,000-plus pages of the *Collected Poems*[1] is a daunting prospect for even the most dedicated reader of Thomas Merton. The sheer number of the poems, the obscurity of many of them, as well as their uneven quality, have tended to keep most Merton readers from acquaintance with more than a handful of the most familiar pieces. Daniel Berrigan, in an oft-quoted comment, said, "He needed a Pound, to cut him to size"[2] (alluding to Ezra Pound's editing of T. S. Eliot's *Waste Land*). Just hefting the book itself might incline us to modify that to: he needed someone to cut it to a pound—even the paperback edition weights three times that. Merton's poetry is probably too heavy, in more than one sense, ever to be popular, yet neglecting it leads to an incomplete and thus distorted understanding of Merton as both writer and person. Although I doubt anyone would claim that his verse is as important as his prose, the fact that Merton, particularly at the outset (1939-1949) and again toward the conclusion (1966-1968) of his writing career, dedicated a considerable portion of the limited time available to him for writing to poetry, and identified himself explicitly, at times even primarily, as a poet, should never be overlooked or minimized.

Merton's verse is both an important resource for discovering and evaluating his developing spiritual and social vision, and a quite significant if secondary contribution to his overall achievement as literary figure and as "spiritual master" (to borrow a term from Lawrence Cunningham's now classic anthology[3]). The poetry, therefore, needs to be recognized as an integral part and not a peripheral dimension of his work. The poetry reinforces and extends themes and ideas found in the prose and provides insights on some topics available nowhere else.

I believe, moreover, that the Collected Poems needs to be read complete, that the whole is greater than the sum of its parts. This is not to say, of course, that unless one is going to read all the poems one should not read any of them—hardly a proposition that will increase the familiarity and popularity of Merton's verse.[4] What I mean, rather, is that patterns of recurring and developing imagery and themes weave their way through the nearly three decades of Merton's verse in such a way that a reading of virtually any poem is enriched by seeing it in the context of these broader patterns.[5] One such pattern that seems to me among the most central and significant for appreciating Merton's poetry can be discerned by noting an apparent coincidence with regard to work dating from the beginning and the end of his career. The last of Merton's separately published volumes of verse, which appeared the year after his death, is entitled The Geography of Lograire.[6] The very first word in the Collected Poems also happens to be "geography": it is found in the four-line epigraph that opens Early Poems (1940-1942): "Geography comes to an end, /Compass has lost all earthly north, /Horizons have no meaning, /Nor roads an explanation."[7] The fact Merton selected these lines to introduce this gathering of previously uncollected early verse (which actually appeared only after his death, in 1971[8]) signals his own recognition of the consistent though multivalent presence of topographical images and themes throughout his verse. This can be seen in such poems as "Landscape: Wheatfields," "Landscape, Prophet and Wild Dog," "Landscape: Beast," or "Aubade: Lake Erie," "The Ohio River—Louisville," "The Trappist Cemetery—Gethsemani," and "Grace's House," yet is by no means restricted to poems with specific locations in their titles. Michael Mott has commented that "It would be hard to exaggerate the importance of place for Thomas Merton,"[9] and this is particularly, though certainly not exclusively, applicable to the poetry. His extraordinary attentiveness to the spatial dimension, to place, not just as setting but as subject—as sacramental revelation of divine creativity; as symbolic manifestation of religious vision; as concrete representation of moral and spiritual alternatives; as "objective correlative" for interior states of mind and soul—is a central aspect of many of his most fully realized poems, from all phases of his career, and provides an important, perhaps the most important, point of access for appreciating the foundation and evaluating the results of Merton's vast poetic enterprise. Therefore this motif is, I believe, one thread that can guide us through the daunting and at times seemingly impenetrable labyrinth of the *Collected Poems*. While in this brief discussion we can do no more than to take samplings of this attentiveness to place, spatiality, "geography," I hope it will be enough to suggest its centrality and significance, and thereby to encourage readers to continue to follow the thread for themselves. Merton's fascination with this pattern is a key which can be of value for many readers.

One can identify three broad categories into which Merton's poetry of place can be assigned, related in a loosely dialectical way: sacramental, desacralized, and interior landscapes. The first mode focuses on the capacity of the created world to manifest the power, wisdom and love of the Creator. "To the true Christian poet," Merton writes, "the whole world and all the incidents of life tend to be sacraments—signs of God, signs of His love working in the world."[10] Merton's extraordinary sensitivity to the natural world allows him to find in creation an epiphany of the Creator. In many of the early poems this sacramentality is expressed through the use of implicitly eucharistic imagery, finding in wheatfields and vineyards signs of the divine presence analogous to, and perfected by, the sacrament of communion. Such awareness is characteristically associated with the innocence of children or the wisdom of saints, who are able to see the world as God intended it to be, to recognize paradise hidden within the ordinary forms of everyday reality, as in the lovely early lyric "Evening,"[11] when the children describe apple trees in springtime as "their innocent sisters, dressed in blossoms, /Still wearing, in the blurring dusk, /White dresses from that morning's first communion":[12] the flowering of the trees, a sign of renewal, is indeed a communion with the creative Lord who gives form and life to all creatures. When Merton enters monastic life the abbey itself frequently serves as an image of this holistic vision, as in poems such as "Trappists, Working," written shortly after his arrival, or "After the Night Office—Gethsemani Abbey,"[13] where the monastery represents the embodiment of a harmonious integration of the natural, the human and the divine and the antithesis to scenes of disorder representing a world that has ignored or rejected God. Later, the desert landscape will provide a paradoxical locus of spiritual fecundity, as in "Macarius and the Pony"[14] or "Night-Flowering Cactus."[15]

Even in these poems of sacramental awareness, there is often a direct or implicit contrast with the perspective of those who fail to perceive the truth because they try to force reality to conform to their own expectations, and many poems juxtapose contrasting scenes which serve as concrete representations of contradictory worldviews: desert and city ("The Flight into Egypt"), or monastery and "world" ("The Trappist Abbey: Matins") or Harlem and Wall Street ("Aubade: Harlem"). The two settings typically embody the Augustinian distinction between self-love and self-gift, *cupiditas* and *caritas*, the City of Man and the City of God, antitheses particularly evident in Merton's verse drama *The Tower of Babel*.

The awareness of a fallen world is evident in the "landscape of disaster" of which Merton writes in his best-known poem, the elegy on the death of his brother John Paul during the Second World War,[16] and in numerous other poems which Merton writes about war both early and late in his career.[17] Frequently the city, with its dehumanizing routines and sharp divisions between rich and poor, epitomizes this desacralized landscape, as in "Aubade—The City"[18] or "Hymn of Not Much Praise for New York City," or in the context of the Civil Rights Movement, "And the Children of Birmingham."[19] But Merton avoids a simplistic dualism in which nature is perceived as good and revelatory while urban life is rejected as profane and distorted. In one of his earliest poems, "The City's Spring," the urban landscape is perceived as having a sacramental capacity of its own, albeit one that is too seldom recognized by its inhabitants. Nor is there anything automatic about the sacramentality of the natural world, which can be unrecognized and undermined by human greed and desire to dominate. Merton was usually wise enough to recognize the danger of creating an oversimplified dualism, dividing people, places, and events into mutually exclusive classifications of good and evil, unduly idealizing the monastery or demonizing the world. He soon recognized that religious life had its flaws and lapses and that no earthly landscape can or should be viewed as a perfect correlative to God's eternal and infinite love. From the mid-1950s, he increasingly used landscape imagery to symbolize interior states, finding the alternatives of good and evil within the self, and replacing condemnation with compassionate identification with the world and its struggles. These poems express the realization that the real journey of life is interior, that the ultimate landscape to be explored is the landscape of the soul, as expressed in the final lines of one of his most significant poems, "Elias—Variations on a Theme":

> Under the blunt pine
> Elias becomes his own geography...
> His own pattern, surrounding the Spirit
> By which he is himself surrounded:
>
> For the free man's road has neither beginning nor end.[20]

A similar perspective marks the concluding sections of *Cables to the Ace*, where Merton, having depicted depersonalized, manipulative, coercive modern society through much of the poem, finally turns to the desert as an alternative: "for each of us there is a point of nowhereness in the middle of movement, a point of nothingness in the midst of being: the incomparable point, not to be discovered by insight. If you seek it you do not find it. If you stop seeking, it is there. But you must not turn to it. Once you become aware of yourself as seeker, you are lost. But if you are content to be lost you will be found without knowing it, precisely because you are lost, for you are, at last, nowhere." Only in this emptiness can the "true word of eternity" be heard that "is spoken only in the spirit of that man who is himself a wilderness."[21]

To get a better sense of how the dynamics of Merton's shifting poetic landscapes actually function in practice, it is helpful to look in detail at representative poems that exemplify each of these three major developments.

**Sacramental awareness**

The best known, and arguably the best, of Merton's poems of sacramental awareness is "Grace's House,"[22] based on a drawing by a young girl whose name could not have been more apt.[23] The poem begins abruptly, with a prepositional phrase, a very effective initial point of focus:

> On the summit: it stands on a fair summit
> Prepared by winds: and solid smoke
> Rolls from the chimney like a snow cloud.
> Grace's house is secure. (ll. 1-4)

The description of the scene literally begins at the top, and using the phrase "*the* summit" has the effect of aligning it with all the other summits of myth, perhaps particularly with Dante's location of Eden at the summit of the seven-storied Mount Purgatory. Only then does the poem drop back from the unmodified description to a subject and verb and the more modest "a fair summit"—from the archetype to a particular, specific exemplification of this archetype. What is being described (prescinding from the title) is not yet specified—in fact at this point the poem looks at the summit from a primordial perspective, a time before "it" was there: the detail "Prepared by winds" is not based directly on the drawing, obviously—it is interpretation rather than description: "winds" are symbolically associated with the creative work of the Holy Spirit, as in the words of Jesus to Nicodemus in John 3:8 (The wind blows where it wills, and you can hear the sound it makes, but you do not know where it comes from or where it goes; so it is with everyone who is born of the Spirit) and the wind/spirit that blows over the waters at the beginning of Genesis. The detail suggests preparation for creation, and implicitly for transformation as well. Attention then shifts not to the house itself but to the smoke coming from the chimney, the first indication that the object being described is in fact a house.[24] But the smoke is not dingy or dirty but "like a snow cloud," an image of purity (which is in fact "solid" white in the drawing). Only at this point, to conclude the first verse paragraph, is full identification made—the description of the house as "secure"—firmly set on its site—recalls the house built on rock at the end of the Sermon on the Mount in Matthew 7. It also creates an interesting parallel with St. John of the Cross's poem "The Dark Night" with its references to the "casa" being "segura" (and even its repeated phrase "Ah, the sheer grace");[25] but this poem is firmly cataphatic, focused on the sacramentality of the scene—here it is not a matter of leaving the house and going forth into the darkness, as in St. John's poem, but rather of reaching the house on the sunlit hill, a reverse dynamic—but it is likely that the language, deliberately or not, reflects that of St. John. There is no effort to elaborate, here or elsewhere in the poem, on the symbolic significance of the girl's name—it is allowed to operate "on its own" without spoiling its effect by foregrounding it too obviously. Much of the effectiveness of this opening section depends on the way the poet weaves together sounds—the assonance of "fair" and "Prepared," of "smoke," "Rolls" and "snow," "cloud" and "house"; the slant rhyme of "stands" and "winds"; the repeated "s" in "summit," "stands," "solid smoke" "snow," moved to the end of words in "Grace's house" and echoed by the unaccented first syllable of "secure." These connections will continue into the opening line of the second section as "Grace's" is connected by assonance with "blade" and consonance with "grass."

In this next section, the focus is on the landscape:

> No blade of grass is not counted,
> No blade of grass forgotten on this hill.
> Twelve flowers make a token garden.
> There is no path to the summit—
> No path drawn
> To Grace's house. (ll. 5-10)

The emphasis on the grass is true to the drawing, which is remarkably thorough in its detailed depiction of each separate blade (counting them all would actually be quite a task!). The implication is that even the apparently least significant objects are to be recognized as important, precious, not to be overlooked. The phrasing of the first statement recalls Christ's words that the hairs of the head are all counted (Matt. 10:30); the repetition with variations serves to reinforce this point. The "Twelve flowers" (actually more than seem to be found in the drawing), with their scriptural echoes, form "a token garden" not just in the sense that they are a part to be taken for the whole but that they are symbolic, a sign of fullness, completion, creating a garden scene suggestive of Eden. The conclusion of this section echoes its opening in that it is also phrased as a repetition with variation. The full implications of this detail are not yet developed; the absence of a path could be considered simply as one more detail of the landscape, perhaps even as evidence of an unintended incompleteness of the scene, as the word "drawn" indicates for the first time that what is being described is, in fact, a picture. But the repetition of the key word "summit" from the opening line, and the line break that turns the second clause (with a syntactic structure exactly parallel to l. 6) into two lines, leaving "To Grace's house" by itself, subtly foreshadows the symbolic significance that this detail will assume at the conclusion of the poem. Once again the sound devices of this section effectively reinforce its sense of unity and order: the perfect iambic pentameter of line 6 gives it particular prominence, and forms a contrast with the trochaic rhythms of the following line's "Twelve flowers make a token garden" (also a pentameter), with its mirroring effect of the "w-l-v"/"f-l-w" of "Twelve flowers," the medial "k" of "make" and "tok-" and the echo of the identical unaccented final syllables of "token" and "garden" (linking as well to "-gotten" in the previous line).

Mention of the house at the end of this section leads naturally to consideration of a particular detail of its appearance to open the following verse paragraph:

> All the curtains are arranged
> Not for hiding but for seeing out.
> In one window someone looks out and winks.
> Two gnarled short
> Fortified trees have knotholes
> From which animals look out.
> From behind a corner of Grace's house
> Another creature peeks out. (ll. 11-18)

There is a certain amount of "expansion" of the drawing here—no wink is evident in the picture (the girl in the window has only dots for eyes); a knothole is visible only in one of the trees; there is only a very sketchy creature, if there is one at all, behind the corner of the house. This entire section is linked by the motif of "seeing out": "someone" from within the house "looks out and winks"; "animals" from within the trees "look out"; a "creature" from behind the house "peeks out." Humans, animals and "creatures" in general are all participating in the common process of seeing—and being seen. There is no hiding, as Adam and Eve did in the garden after their sin. The "wink" of the figure in the window suggests eye contact and even a signal of sorts to the viewer. What all the participants share is both being fully integrated into the scene and yet being able to look out from it—the "innocent 'outgazing' proper to the child" or of the "animal [which] simply 'gazes out' without any consciousness of a center which gazes" that Rilke describes: "the 'pure consciousness' of Zen, the consciousness that has not fallen into self-consciousness, separateness, and spectatorship," which "does not look *at* things, and does not ignore them, annihilate them, negate them" but "accepts them fully, in complete oneness with them. It looks 'out of them,' as though fulfilling the role of consciousness not for itself only but *for them also*."[26] Once again sound reinforces sense: again there is a regular iambic pentameter (without the initial unaccented syllable) in the second line of the section; "winks" echoes both "win-" and "looks" earlier in the line; "creature" is linked both to "corner" in the previous line by its "c" and "r" sounds and to "peeks" by assonance. The cluster of accented syllables in "Two gnarled short / Fort-" (with the rhyme connecting the lines) reinforces the impression of sturdiness here (in the context "Fortified" suggests not defensiveness but something substantial, strong [cf. the root "*fortis*"], firm, parallel to the "secure" of the house).

While this section with its multiple figures was panoramic, what follows focuses on a single creature:

> Important: hidden in the foreground
> Most carefully drawn
> The dog smiles, his foreleg curled, his eye like an aster.
> Nose and collar are made with great attention:
> This dog is loved by Grace! (ll. 19-23)

The phrase "hidden in the foreground" seems paradoxical, but is quite accurate: the dog is fully integrated into the scene—not standing out as separate from his surroundings—perhaps suggestive of the puzzles of finding concealed objects in children's activity books; yet while "hidden" he is not "hiding"—there is no concealment, just a need for discernment on the viewer's part. He is "most carefully drawn"—presented as unique. The reference to his "eye like an aster" (which is indeed quite prominent in the drawing) relates the dog both to the outseeing creatures of the previous section and to the flowers of the section before that, and as "aster" is also linked etymologically to "star" there may be a suggestion of a parallel with celestial light here also. The care and attention of the drawing are perceived as a sign of love, of a world marked by love, the love of the artist for her dog, whose smile reciprocates, and by analogy of the Creator for the creature. The "musical" dimension of the verse continues, as "collar" echoes both "aster" and "curled" and "made" and "great" are linked with "Grace" by assonance, and in the latter case by alliteration as well.

The section that follows provides the first reference to the world beyond the hill, beyond the drawing:

> And there: the world!
> Mailbox number 5
> Is full of Valentines for Grace.
> There is a name on the box, name of a family
> Not yet ready to be written in language. (ll. 24-28)

The initial detail here focuses more on connections than on distinctions. The mailbox (which is part of the drawing) is filled with valentines (which are not seen—there is no way to see what is inside the mailbox) that represent the wider world's love for the little girl, or perhaps the girl's perception of the wider world as loving: there is a sense of harmony and attraction linking the two. At the same time, the mailbox preserves a sense of mystery, of difference, for the unreadable name is an indication that no label is adequate to express her identity, which transcends the limits of language.

In the lines that follow, the distinction between the two realms begins to be recognized and its implications to be considered:

> A spangled arrow there
> Points from our Coney Island
> To her green sun-hill. (ll. 29-31)

The "arrow" refers to the flag on the mailbox, which actually is arrow-shaped, and does point toward the hill. "Coney Island" is of course outside the frame of the picture, as it is outside the experience of the artist. The archetypal amusement park, Coney Island with its noise, its crowds and its frenetic pace is an icon of triviality, of busyness without purpose, a symbol of contemporary culture's obsession with diversion. This is the world of "experience" in the Blakean sense, juxtaposed with the child's world of innocence, the hill bathed in light and filled with the natural vitality of creation.

The distinction between "our Coney Island" and "her green sun-hill" is further developed in the section that follows:

> Between our world and hers
> Runs a sweet river:
> (No, it is not the road,
> It is the uncrossed crystal
> Water between our ignorance and her truth.) (ll. 32-36)

Located at the very bottom of the picture, the stream does indeed form the border between the world of the drawing, the visionary world of the child, and the world of the observer. It is reminiscent of the River Jordan as the boundary of the Promised Land, and perhaps of the river that separates the narrator from the young girl in the medieval dream-vision *Pearl* (though Grace, unlike the pearl maiden, is alive) or the river Lethe that must be passed to enter into paradise in Dante's *Purgatorio*. Its "uncrossed crystal" water is a symbol of purity, and with its likely wordplay on "cross" and "Christ" suggests a vision of paradise before the fall, before sin and death, before the necessity of the cross. The speaker says it separates "our ignorance and her truth," but one might have expected the converse: she is still ignorant of the reality of the fallen world and its evils, while we know what reality is actually like. But the point is that Grace is still able to grasp intuitively what creation is intended to be, to see the world as God made it; she retains a holistic vision that we have lost, because it is inaccessible to the analytic mind; it can be known only from within, through love and wisdom, relational and participatory knowledge.

The lines that follow, which finally make explicit the identification that the speaker's description has suggested from the outset, move the focus back to the scene itself:

> O paradise, O child's world!
> Where all the grass lives
> And all the animals are aware!
> The huge sun, bigger than the house
> Stands and streams with life in the east

> While in the west a thunder cloud
> Moves away forever. (ll. 37-43)

Following the initial revelatory invocation here, the edenic landscape is epitomized in terms of plant and animal life—the grass is alive, the animals aware. The speaker then immediately reverts to the concrete details of the drawing, effectively countering any tendency to abstraction or grandiose pronouncements. He returns to the top of the drawing, to the rising sun in the east, sign and source of life, symbol of new beginnings. The sun is indeed "huge" in the drawing—in fact only a quarter arc is seen in the upper left-hand corner; this is definitely a depiction of a "mysticism of light." While the sun "stands and streams with life" (paralleling the "sweet river" at the bottom of the page), the thunder cloud "[m]oves away forever": one remains as a permanent reality, the other is disappearing (literally, as it too bleeds beyond the edge of the drawing). These contrasting images, more "cosmic" than the details of the description of the hill itself, have apparently been reserved for this point in the poem as all-encompassing symbols of the two contrasting, indeed incompatible worldviews that have emerged in the previous sections.

The poet signals that the poem is drawing to a close by providing a recapitulation with variations of the opening lines of the second section:

> No blade of grass is not blessed
> On this archetypal, cosmic hill,
> This womb of mysteries. (ll. 44-46)

The grass that was "counted" in line 5 is now "blessed"—by the sunlight, but more fundamentally by the Creator, who cares for even the most ordinary components of creation; "on this hill" (l. 6) becomes "on this archetypal, cosmic hill"—recognized as representative of all the high places where the divine is encountered, and as a microcosm of the entire universe as it was intended to be. As the "womb of mysteries" it is, like Eden, the source of further life, but also the source of insight into the mystery of reality, the hidden wholeness of creation that is always present beneath the surface yet generally ignored or denied.

Again there is a movement from these more universal images to more specific and concrete details, which counters any hint of pretentiousness, while at the same time completing the recapitulation of the entire drawing from top (sun, thunder cloud) through middle (grassy hillside) to bottom:

> I must not omit to mention a rabbit
> And two birds, bathing in the stream
> Which is no road... (ll. 47-49)

In these almost final lines, the speaker refers to himself directly for the first time in the poem—calling attention to himself would have been a distraction earlier. He seems to be reminding himself as he approaches the conclusion that he needs to include mention of these particular creatures as part of the scene, but in the process he is returning the focus to the stream, which is not a barrier for the innocent animals as it is for fallen humans, and which is once again (as in line 34) identified as "no road," a declaration that prepares the way for the final line, which stands by itself: "...because // Alas, there is no road to Grace's house!" (ll. 49-50). This line is also a variation on earlier descriptive detail (ll. 8-10), but repeated now with a sense of its full significance, and with the first interjection of an affective response in the initial "Alas," concluding the poem with an apparent sense of loss and regret. One may ask, then, if the poem is finally pessimistic, if it presents a vision of paradise only to admit its complete inaccessibility. Certainly, the lack of a road means there is no "way" to return to Eden, no method, no set of plans or directions. A clear path would indicate the possibility of reaching this perfection by one's own efforts. Yet it is, after all, the house of Grace that is on the summit, which cannot be reached through a self-directed journey, cannot be achieved or earned, but is nevertheless available as sheer gift for those who are willing to be led along a road which is no road, a pathless path to paradise.

### Counter-sacramentality

In Merton's poetic vision the possibility of failing to recognize and respond to the revelatory power of the natural world becomes actual in the early poem entitled "The Regret,"[27] which describes a failure to make connections, a "counter-sacramentality," in its depiction of human alienation from the rhythms and patterns of creation.

The opening line stands alone, separated from the rest of the poem like the personified figure it describes: "When cold November sits among the reeds like an unlucky fisher" (l. 1). The image is one of isolation, discomfort, futility, failure. What follows indicates that it is less an objective description than a projection of the speaker's own feelings about the season:

> And ducks drum up as sudden as the wind
> Out of the rushy river,
> We slowly come, robbed of our rod and gun,
> Walking amid the stricken cages of the trees. (ll. 2-5)

The juxtaposition of the hapless fisherman with the flock of ducks suggests that he would be better off hunting than fishing, but the speaker and his companions (presumably his audience) are deprived of both rod and gun, powerless to catch any game at all. The imagery used here reveals why the human figures are out of sympathy with the seasonal round. There is a sense of being aggrieved and resentful at the turn of events, but the fault lies not with nature but with the misperception of humans' relationship to nature: the equation of trees with cages suggests that nature is regarded not as a sacrament, a gift, but as a possession, something to be captured and kept under control.

Merton's speaker's frustration is that the effort to cage up nature, to consider oneself its owner or keeper, is inevitably thwarted by the patterns of the temporal cycle. The enemy is transience, mutability. He has been "robbed" of rod and gun, but robbed more fundamentally of the world of summer, the pleasant weather, the "good life." But this is evidence of a distorted perception of the world: trees are not cages, and they are certainly not "stricken," a word that suggests not only "damaged" but "diseased." The dis-ease is in the speaker's own mind. Caged birds may be restricted in their movements, but those in the trees are free to follow their instinctive urge to migrate, and there is no way for humans to prevent their disappearance.

In the opening lines of the following stanza, the image is altered from keeping in to keeping out, but with no more successful results:

> The stormy weeks have all gone home like drunken hunters,
> Leaving the gates of the grey world wide open to December.
> But now there is no speech of branches in these broken jails. (ll. 6-8)

Here the "stormy weeks" are faulted for their carelessness in failing to bar the gates to the approaching winter, imaged as a sort of unwelcome trespasser. But in fact this "explanation" for the arrival of December is merely evidence of the speaker's refusal to accept the processes of nature. So long as the trees are considered as "broken jails," from which imprisoned creatures have fled, it is little wonder that there is "no speech" to be heard there, no revelation of the true significance of the events being described. The consequence of this narrowness of vision is apparent in the lines that follow, perhaps the central pivot of the entire poem, coming as they do at its midpoint:

> Acorns lie over the earth, no less neglected
> Than our unrecognizable regret:
> And here we stand as senseless as the oaks,
> As dumb as elms. (ll. 9-12)

The speaker considers the acorns scattered beneath the trees to be neglected, but in fact he himself is ignoring the developmental potential of the acorns, which are of course seeds, signs of new life to come; they have not been simply discarded but left to germinate and so to participate in the rhythm of renewal, of seasonal death and rebirth. To all this the speaker is deaf. His human regret is thus "unrecognizable" because it does not correspond to the dynamism of creation—it is out of harmony with the rhythms of the year. He claims to find an analogue for his inarticulate grief in the "dumb" and "senseless" trees, no longer filled with the song of birds or even the rustling of the leaves, but in fact the correspondence is suspect: the oaks and elms may still have something to communicate, even with their limbs stripped and seemingly dead, but the speaker's state of mind makes it virtually impossible for him to be receptive.

This sense of alienation grows more intense in the lines that follow:

> And though we seem as grave as jailers, yet we did not come to wonder
> Who picked the locks of the past days, and stole our summer.
> (We are no longer listeners for curious saws, and secret keys!) (ll. 13-15)

Here he admits defeat, renouncing even the role of jailer: not only will he no longer try to impede time's passage, he will make no effort to determine how the summer has disappeared. This is not an expression of resignation and acceptance, but of despondent submission. The line break allows the words "we did not come to wonder" to stand momentarily alone, forming a statement much more accurate than the speaker realizes. It is precisely the lack of wonder, of awe and fascination before the mystery of creation that isolates him from the scene he describes. He rejects the coming winter because of the reminder it brings of his own subjection to time, his own mortality, but it is all to no avail: he is already "as grave as jailers," already carrying death around within him in the form of his fear. Seeing only the forces of death and dissolution in the passage of time, he misses the deeper force of renewal, just as his professed disinterest in the "curious saws" and "secret keys" which made possible the summer's flight obscures his more significant failure to attend to these elements in their more profound sense, the enigmatic sayings and mysterious hidden wisdom (even expressed, perhaps, in musical form) through which the authentic meaning of natural processes would be revealed.

This psychic abasement reaches its lowest point in the final quatrain, where all distinctions between summer and winter, life and death, are obliterated:

> We are indifferent to seasons,
> And stand like hills, deaf.
> And never hear the last of the escaping year
> Go ducking through the bended branches like a leaf. (ll. 16-19)

He has passed from regret to indifference, a loss of faith leading to, or disguised as, a lack of concern. The claim is being made that in doing so he has actually aligned himself fully with nature, represented by the hills, which is just as insensible as he now is. He has accepted a view of the material world as meaningless, a sign of nothing but the absurdity of existence, and has adopted a stance of insensibility. But the final lines suggest that this is a pose, an effort of self-protection designed to spare him the necessity of noticing the end of the year. But the fact that the year is still being described as "escaping" suggests that his earlier possessive attitude is not in fact dissipated, and that a satisfactory solution to his problem will not come through a specious indifference, but only by his honestly recognizing the sources of his regret, and coming to a belief that from his own inner emptiness, no less than from the scattered acorns, new life can sprout. Yet the poem ends with no indication that such a development will take place, other than the implicit recognition that with the departure of the old year comes the simultaneous entrance of the new. But if a person ignores the one, he will miss the other as well. "The Regret," then, depicts the lack of a sacramental consciousness, the refusal or inability to recognize nature as a gift from and a sign of the Creator, and the consequent bitterness and isolation that such a position inevitably entails. Its bleak despair heightens by contrast an appreciation of what authentic sacramentality should be.

**The world as God intended**
Despite its title, Merton's "The Fall"[28] is not simply about the desacralized landscape but about how to reverse the effects of the fall, how and where to encounter the world as God intended it to be. Its opening lines, a single sentence with no less than four negatives, are certainly an expression par excellence of the apophatic approach, the way of negation:

> There is no where in you a paradise that is no place and there
> You do not enter except without a story. (ll. 1-2)

The very beginning of the sentence seems to be saying that paradise is not to be found within "you," but this impression is immediately countered by the clause modifying "paradise," which indicates that "no where" is not to be equated with "nowhere" but with "no place": the inner paradise is not present as a specified, distinct location that can be defined, pinpointed, mapped out—it is, nevertheless, "there" in some mysterious way, but cannot be entered "except without a story"—only by a radical self-surrender, by stripping away the illusion of one's own autonomy, by letting go of the story we have invented in order to provide for ourselves an identity over which we exercise control, can "paradise" be re-entered.

This negative language continues through the succeeding lines:

> To enter there is to become unnameable.
> Whoever is there is homeless for he has no door and
>   no identity with which to go out and to come in.
> Whoever is nowhere is nobody, and therefore cannot
>   exist except as unborn:
> No disguise will avail him anything. (ll. 3-6)

If renouncing one's "story" is the necessary precondition for the recovery of paradise, becoming "unnameable" is the consequence. According to the poet one becomes not merely "unnamed" but "unnameable"—indefinable, not reducible to a label, to a limited identity. One is homeless because the distinction between one's home and everywhere else has become insignificant; there are no doors because all divisions between inside and outside, here and there, are transcended. Paradise has no boundaries, no borders, and to be in paradise is to have no identity that separates or isolates one from anyone else. It is a rediscovery, a reintegration, of the self-in-God, the true self known by God from all eternity, prior to all separation from its divine source and from the rest of creation. It is, as Merton will later say, "beyond the shadow and the disguise,"[29] beyond the masks one creates to assume an artificial identity. "Such a one," the speaker declares, "is neither lost nor found" (l. 7), for such dualistic categories are inapplicable to paradise, to a world of primordial all-embracing unity.

In contrast, to be exiled from Eden is to live in a world of organized routines and recorded identities, subject to divisive labels and categories:

"But he who has an address is lost" (l. 8). To have an address is to have both a place and a name (by which one is "addressed"), which in conventional terms is precisely not to be lost—it is to have and to know one's place and one's identity, to belong, to fit in, to possess a sense of contentment and self-satisfaction. But what is lost here is a sense of participation in a reality that transcends the individual self. This is the "fall" of the poem's title:

> They fall, they fall into apartments and are securely established!
> They find themselves in streets. They are licensed
> To proceed from place to place
> They now know their own names
> They can name several friends and know
> Their own telephones must some time ring. (ll. 9-14)

Merton's wordplay on "apartments," with its connotations of isolation and alienation, highlights the contrast with the "homeless" yet integrated state of paradisal existence. Such "security" may seem reassuring, but its overtones suggest a loss of freedom and openness, a kind of imprisonment (cf. "maximum security") as part of the "establishment"—a static, confined existence. The self that is "found" in the streets (and so, as both lost and found, is doubly distinguished from the paradisal self) is the social self, a superficial identity defined by an accepted and acceptable role in society. The understated sardonic social commentary of being "licensed" to move about (suggesting an extreme dependence on the automobile), of "know[ing] their own names," accepting an identity and role assigned by society, of having the ability to "name several friends" (with no implication that this ability to name represents more than the most superficial knowledge) and of waiting for the telephone to ring, indicating a craving for communication and community that is perpetually disappointed but never relinquished, leads to the parody of oneness created "If all telephones ring at once, if all names are shouted at once and all cars crash at one crossing" (l. 15), a pseudo-unity that is meaningless, incomprehensible and ultimately destructive. It foreshadows the ultimate sharing in a common fate of apocalyptic destruction when "all cities explode and fly away in dust" (l. 16), yet even in such a catastrophe the bureaucracy and its mania for labels will survive: "identities refuse to be lost. There is a name and number for everyone" (l. 17). Such an existence is truly a culture of death, and is most perfectly realized in the efficient organization of the dead, who after all are completely compliant with established routines:

> There is a definite place for bodies, there are pigeon holes for
>     ashes:
> Such security can business buy! (ll. 18-19)

Apparently projecting the past history of the Nazi death camps, with their obsessively careful records, into some future atomic holocaust, the speaker explicitly links the "security" previously associated with having a place to live with having a place to die, or rather to be assigned postmortem; not even nuclear annihilation will eliminate the tendency to "pigeon hole" people—to be carried on, perhaps, by computers properly programmed to keep accurate lists of the dead.

While the poem thus far seems to have set up an antithesis between interior and societal landscapes, personal and social identities, it concludes by transcending such a distinction, and revealing that only those who have been liberated from oppressive social identities are truly able to live authentically and creatively in the social world without being trapped and dehumanized by it:

> Who would dare to go nameless in so secure a universe?
> Yet, to tell the truth, only the nameless are at home in it.
> They bear with them in the center of nowhere
>     the unborn flower of nothing:
> This is the paradise tree. It must remain unseen until words end
>     and arguments are silent. (ll. 20-23)

To be nameless in such a world is to be truly free because one evades all classifications and restrictions. Paradoxically, only those who are "homeless" (l. 3), completely detached, can be "at home" in a fallen world, because they alone find their center not in the plausible but fraudulent order of a "secure" social environment but in the genuine security of knowing creation as an epiphany of divine love. The vulnerability of namelessness, which has no self-image to maintain and defend, provides the only reliable protection against both interior and exterior pressures to conform to distorted and malignant definitions of person and society. Only the nameless can draw on resources that liberate them from the need to know, and keep, their place in society; only they "bear with them...the unborn flower of nothing," not an object to be possessed or analyzed or distinguished from other objects but the eternal and everlasting mystery at the center of existence, the tree of life, "the paradise tree" that is always present but unperceived, to be revealed only when all attempts to define and explain it, and so to possess it, are relinquished.

Thus, for Thomas Merton, interior and exterior landscapes are ultimately recognized as not alternative but correlative, not contradictory but complementary, but only for those whose interior exploration has led to the discovery that no specific setting can be more than an emblem of the divine presence, that to be nowhere is to be in touch with everywhere, that transcendence is not the opposite of immanence but its necessary precondition, that "There is no where in you a paradise that is no place," that "the surest home is pointless" (*Cables to the Ace*)[30]—an uncharted center which opens out on the fathomless abyss of divine creative love.

It is the process of recognizing that "pointless" point, of following the pathless path, of "getting nowhere," that is the fundamental dynamic of Merton's "landscape" poems in particular, and of his poetry as whole. For when "you are, at last, nowhere" (the epiphanic moment of *Cables to the Ace*) you are at last open to *everywhere* (the central recognition of *The Geography of Lograire*) because you have encountered the Presence that is the Ground and Goal of all reality.

**Notes**

1. Merton, Thomas, *Collected Poems* (New York: New Directions, 1977); for an overview of this volume, and summaries of the individual volumes of Merton's verse, see Shannon, William H., Christine M. Bochen, and Patrick F. O'Connell, *The Thomas Merton Encyclopedia* (Maryknoll, NY: Orbis, 2002).
2. Berrigan, Daniel SJ, "The Seventy Times Seventy-Seven Storey Mountain," *Cross Currents* 27 (Winter, 1977-1978), p. 93.
3. Cunningham, Lawrence S., ed., *Thomas Merton: Spiritual Master* (New York: Paulist, 1992).

4. For an excellent new selection of Merton's poetry, arranged thematically, see Merton, Thomas, *In the Dark before Dawn: New Selected Poems*, ed. Lynn Szabo (New York: New Directions, 2005).

5. Commentators on this material have provided helpful orientations to some of these patterns. George Woodcock, one of the first critics to integrate a discussion of Merton's verse into a broad consideration of his work, distinguished between "poetry of the choir," the rather ornate, liturgically influenced products of Merton's early years in the monastery, and "poetry of the desert," the much more austere verse of the last decade of his life: see his *Thomas Merton, Monk and Poet* (New York: Farrar, Straus, Giroux, 1978), pp. 51-62 and 74-86. George Kilcourse has added the categories of "poetry of the forest," characteristic of pieces written from Merton's hermitage, and "poetry of paradise consciousness," works that captured the primordial innocence and unity of creation; see his *Ace of Freedoms: Thomas Merton's Christ* (Notre Dame, IN: University of Notre Dame Press, 1993), p. 44, pp. 56-87. Lynn Szabo has explored the paradoxical interplay between efforts at verbal articulation and awareness of the divine reality beyond the expression of language; see her "The Sound of Sheer Silence: A Study of the Poetics of Thomas Merton," *The Merton Annual* 13 (2000), pp. 208-21. Malgorzata Poks has emphasized the thematic continuities in Merton's verse in her "Thomas Merton's Poetry of Endless Inscription: A Tale of Liberation and Expanding Horizons," *The Merton Annual* 14 (2001), pp. 184-222.

6. Merton, Thomas, *The Geography of Lograire* (New York: New Directions, 1969).

7. *Collected Poems*, p. 2; these lines are taken from the final poem in the collection, given the title "Sacred Heart 2 (A Fragment...)" (*Collected Poems*, p. 24).

8. Merton, Thomas, *Early Poems: 1940-1942* (Lexington, KY: Anvil Press, 1971).

9. Mott, Michael, *The Seven Mountains of Thomas Merton* (Boston: Houghton Mifflin, 1984), p. 205.

10. Merton, Thomas, *The Literary Essays of Thomas Merton*, ed. Patrick Hart, OCSO (New York: New Directions, 1981), p. 345.

11. For a discussion of this and related poems, see O'Connell, Patrick F., "Sacrament and Sacramentality in Thomas Merton's *Thirty Poems*," in *The Vision of Thomas Merton*, ed. Patrick F. O'Connell (Notre Dame, IN: Ave Maria Press, 2003), pp. 155-84.

12. *Collected Poems*, p. 42.

13. For a discussion of this and related poems, see O'Connell, Patrick F., "Thomas Merton's Wake-Up Calls: Aubades and Monastic Dawn Poems from *A Man in the Divided Sea*," *The Merton Annual* 12 (1999), pp. 129-63.

14. For a discussion of this and its companion poem, see O'Connell, Patrick F., "More Wisdom of the Desert: Thomas Merton's Macarius Poems." *Cistercian Studies Quarterly*, 40.3 (2005), pp. 253-78.

15. For a discussion of this and related poems, see Thurston, Bonnie B., "Wrestling with Angels: Some Mature Poems of Thomas Merton," *Vision of Thomas Merton*, pp. 187-201; and O'Connell, Patrick F., "Nurture by Nature: Emblems of Stillness in a Season of Fury," *The Merton Annual* 21 (2008) [in press].

16. For a discussion of this poem, see O'Connell, Patrick F., "Grief Transfigured: Merton's Elegy on His Brother," *The Merton Seasonal* 18:1 (Winter, 1993), pp. 10-15.

17. For a discussion of the early poems on war, see O'Connell, Patrick F., "Landscapes of Disaster: Thomas Merton's War Poems," *The Merton Annual* 19 (2006), pp. 178-233.
18. For a discussion of this and related poems see "Thomas Merton's Wake-Up Calls."
19. For a discussion of this and related poems see O'Connell, Patrick F., "The Civil Rights Poetry of Thomas Merton," *Across the Rim of Chaos: Thomas Merton's Prophetic Vision* (Stratton-on-the-Fosse, Radstock: Thomas Merton Society of Great Britain and Ireland, 2005), pp. 89-113.
20. *Collected Poems*, p. 245; for a discussion of this poem, see O'Connell, Patrick F., "The Geography of Solitude: Thomas Merton's 'Elias—Variations on a Theme,'" *The Merton Annual* 1 (1988), pp. 151-90.
21. *Collected Poems*, pp. 452-53.
22. *Collected Poems*, pp. 330-31.
23. For background to the poem, see Merton's letter of August 2, 1962 to Elbert Sisson, Grace's father, in Merton, Thomas, *The Road to Joy: Letters to New and Old Friends*, ed. Robert E. Daggy (New York: Farrar, Straus, Giroux, 1989), pp. 323-24; see also the letter of August 9, 1962 to Mark Van Doren (*Road to Joy*, p. 45) and a letter of May 13, 1967 to Grace Sisson herself about a later drawing (*Road to Joy*, pp. 352-53).
24. In "When Is a Building Beautiful?" (*New York Review of Books* 54.4 [15 March 2007], pp. 19-21), Alison Lurie writes, "There was also a generic type of benevolent dwelling that appeared in our art, of the type that the French philosopher Gaston Bachelard speaks of in *The Poetics of Space* as the picture most frequently drawn by the very young, that picture sometimes called the 'Happy House.' This is the image, familiar to almost every parent or teacher, of a square one- or two-story home with a peaked roof, a central door, and two or more symmetrically placed windows that may sometimes suggest a face with eyes and a mouth. In cool climates, the house often has a chimney with curls of smoke pouring out, suggesting that the building is warm and inhabited. Frequently the Happy House is surrounded by trees and/or flowers, and a big yellow sun shines in the sky, which is indicated by a strip of bright blue at the top of the drawing" (pp. 19-20). Despite the striking similarity, Merton had not yet read Bachelard's discussion of the "Happy House" at the time of writing "Grace's House." In "Merton's Hermitage: Bachelard, Domestic Space, and Spiritual Transformation" (*Spiritus* 4.2 [Fall, 2004], pp. 123-50), Belden Lane notes that Merton "enthusiastically read" *The Poetics of Space* while living at the hermitage (p. 124); for Merton's own comments on Bachelard see the journal entries for September 30 and October 2, 3, and 8, 1967 (Merton, Thomas, *Learning to Love: Exploring Solitude and Freedom. Journals, vol. 6: 1966-1967*, ed. Christine M. Bochen [San Francisco: HarperCollins, 1997], pp. 295, 296, 298, and 300).
25. *The Collected Works of St. John of the Cross*, trans. Kieran Kavanaugh, OCD and Otilio Rodriguez, OCD (Garden City, NY: Doubleday, 1964), p. 711.
26. Merton, Thomas, *Mystics and Zen Masters* (New York: Farrar, Straus and Giroux, 1967), pp. 244-45.
27. *Collected Poems*, p. 33.
28. *Collected Poems*, pp. 354-55.
29. Merton, Thomas, *The Asian Journal*, ed. Naomi Burton Stone, Brother Patrick Hart and James Laughlin (New York: New Directions, 1973), p. 236.
30. *Collected Poems*, p. 454.

# "LOVE FOR THE PARADISE MYSTERY"
## Thomas Merton: Contemplative Ecologist

Kathleen Deignan

"Love for the paradise mystery"[1] is a dominant motif woven through all the writings of Thomas Merton—a gossamer thread of mystical insight and prophetic urgency that fastens together the assemblage of his multi-focused literary legacy. Now, forty years after his death, a pentimento pattern of ecological consciousness becomes evident throughout his corpus as its complexity and unity become more transparent with time. As the contemporary ecological crisis deepens, we urgently require more than instrumental remedies to stem the life-loss of our ecosphere suffered at human hands. We need a penetrating understanding of the more troubling and mysterious pathology underlying it: why, indeed, have we plundered paradise? This was the difficult "koan" Merton carried to fruition over a half-century ago, as he explored the congenital disorientation of spirit that exiles us from our Edenic home in the community of creation. Having suffered such exile, he recovered from it, and taught a holistic therapy of contemplative living that can restore our paradisal consciousness, conscience, and practice. "Here is an unspeakable secret: paradise is all around us and we do not understand. It is wide open .... 'Wisdom,' cries the dawn deacon, but we do not attend."[2]

The wisdom that focused Merton's attention on the encompassing mystery of paradise was a wisdom based on love: "love for the wilderness and for its secret laws."[3] The biblical mythologem of "paradise" served as the foundational archetype grounding his wide-ranging discourse on matters of the sacred, providing a metaphorical way to speak of metaphysical truth: "the world ... made as a temple, a paradise, into which God Himself would descend to dwell familiarly with the spirits He had placed there to tend it for Him."[4] Employing a Cistercian hermeneutic, he interpreted the biblical narrative as a perennial meditation on the gift and loss and recovery of paradise.

> The early chapters of Genesis ... are precisely a poetic and symbolic revelation of God's view of the universe and of His intentions for man. The point of these beautiful chapters is that God made the world as a garden in which He himself took delight. He made man and gave to man the task of sharing in His own divine care for created things. He made man in His own image and likeness, as an artist, a worker, homo faber, as the gardener of paradise.[5]

Entrusted with the earthly paradise of Eden, Adam and Eve—our mythological progenitors—would not simply be another species among the "innocent nations" of the biosphere, but collaborators with God in "governing paradise."[6] Their partnership was so intimate that the Creator entrusted to these earthlings the naming and knowing of all living things.[7] Such confidential governance implied a dimension of primordial familiarity with the Edenic tribes—an acquaintance at once simple, primitive, religious, and non-violent—which sustained a clear vision of the singular vestige of God in the great multiplicity of creatures.[8] Paradise, then, is a dialectical or bi-valent mystery arising in at least two dimensions simultaneously: at once manifesting in the physical sphere of inexhaustive cosmogenesis; and then emerging *within* the noosphere of human consciousness.[9] In Merton's mind, "paradise" is an ontological truth which has an epistemological challenge; it is our vocation, our existential labor, to awaken to "paradise all around us."

**Awakening to paradise**

Merton spent his whole monastic life teaching ways to awaken the paradise mind by the practice of contemplation, a process of deepening subjectivity to access the wellsprings of inherent wisdom. For him, contemplation is the pinnacle of human realization: "It is life itself fully awake, fully active, fully aware that it is alive ... It is gratitude for life, for awareness, for being."[10] In contemplative therapy, the psyche researches its own depths in solitude and silence; the senses rest in a cloister of habitual containment and contentment, purified for the work of beholding and befriending the wonders of embodiment. By experientially touching the source of Being ceaselessly breathing within us, we begin to recognize its sweetness and purity conspiring with all forms of life. Trading breath for breath, the work of recovering paradise unfolds in a mutual sense of indwelling: creature within the Creator; Creator within the creature. Biophilic respect for incarnate divinity reawakens with this Edenic restoration, as the contemplative learns to see in "all visible things an invisible fecundity, a dimmed light, a meek namelessness, a hidden wholeness."[11] Contemplation, then, is the sacred therapeutic practice which evokes and nurtures paradise mind, a cultivated wisdom that rises up in wordless gentleness and flows to all creation: "... at once my own being, my own nature, and the Gift of my Creator's Thought and Art within me, speaking as Hagia Sophia, speaking as my sister, Wisdom."[12]

Merton's joy in the vivid experience of an encompassing Eden, however, suffered the cross beam of anguish at humankind's capacity to miss it, run from it, refuse it, wreck it. "The creative love of God was met, at first, by the destructive and self-centered refusal of man: an act of such incalculable consequences that it would have amounted to the destruction of God's plan, if that were possible."[13] Throughout his literary corpus one hears a profound lamentation for humanity's refusal to be with God the governors and gardeners of paradise, choosing instead a vocation of desecration and de-creation.[14] In stark language he speaks of the inversion of human consciousness—the loss of paradise mind—which constitutes our fall into amnesia of our edenic neighborhood, giving rise to a sense of separation and isolation from the community of creation. The fruit of this alienation is wholesale death by way of murder—murder of the eco-sphere, and even the murder of God, not so much by willful malice as by a new code of perverse consciousness.

> The specific characteristic of this new consciousness, which if not the scientific consciousness is nonetheless a scientific consciousness, is that it excludes the kind of wisdom and initiation we have discovered...by identification, an intersubjective knowledge, a

> communion in cosmic awareness and in nature...a wisdom based on love ... apprehended almost unconsciously in the forest; love for the "spirits" of the wilderness and of the cosmic parent (both Mother and Father)....[15]

Our species has forgotten our true name and nature, our true home and vocation. Centering ourselves on ourselves we have lost our center in Being Itself; therefore we do not know who and what and where we really are. Like Prometheus and the Prodigal—two other recurring themes in Merton's work—we resort to stealing from God the inheritance of vital being that is freely and unfailingly given.[16] This confusion, a self-inversion, constitutes our existential crisis, our deepest disorientation as we run from the source of life to our own productions and generations of fictitious existence. Squandering ourselves in a fragmenting disbursement of consciousness, we fall into dysfunctional unconsciousness—a mindless, trustless, fearful, and rapacious pursuit of life, destructive of our own and Earth's well-being. Like a voice in the wilderness of our self-wrought desolation, Merton cries out for the recovery of our paradise mind and home-ground through the work of contemplative conversion.

> Take thought ... Take thought ... Take thought of the game you have forgotten. You are the child of a great and peaceful race ... an unutterable fable. You were discovered on a mild mountain. You have come up out of the godlike ocean. You are holy, disarmed, signed with a chaste emblem. You are also marked with forgetfulness. Deep inside your breast you wear the number of loss. Take thought ... Do this. Do this. Recover your original name.[17]

### Recovering paradise

The Christian tradition finds in Thomas Merton both a narrator and a narrative of ways to recover paradise. He spent his life listening with his whole sensorium to the voice of the Word Incarnate spelling itself out in the inexhaustive creativity of an unfolding universe. What he heard with the ear of his heart was the song of a cosmos reverberating the glory and wonder of Being, inviting us into experiential communion by thanksgiving and praise. Merton's attendance to the mystery of paradise began early in life, fostered by the aesthetic instruction of his parents, Owen Merton and Ruth Jenkins, both landscape artists. His mother records in her baby book of Tom's development, that he had from infancy a near ecstatic response to the natural world, singing pagan hymns of praise to sun and river and cloud,[18] a form of ecstatic utterance that would become a signature of his nature writing: "For my part my name is that sky, those fence-posts, and those cedar trees ...."[19]

His father Owen mentored Tom's childhood practice of natural contemplation by modeling a vivid, intense, and reverent way of looking at the world, and a disciplined capacity to observe the natural environment with patience and discrimination.[20] This inherently sacramental way of beholding reality was also conditioned by his Welch Celtic temperament, the acknowledgement of which in later life helped him understand his passion for words, woods, and wilderness. It inspired his openness to a hierophanic cosmos where the radiant Spirit was palpably perceived as animating and manifesting throughout creation. It accounted for his parallax vision of spiritual and bodily realities interweaving and interlacing themselves "like manuscript illuminations in the Book of Kells."[21] It inspired his own quest for the earthly paradise sought by his Celtic monastic ancestors who set themselves adrift in skin boats on wild seas in search of their place of resurrection.[22]

Such naturalist sensibilities were made more explicit by his encounter with the Franciscan tradition during his time at Columbia University in the late 1930s, particularly in his academic *lectio* of the great Franciscan theologians Bonaventure and Duns Scotus. Their elucidation of the vestiges or footprints of divinity patterning the natural world gave metaphysical depth to Merton's experience of physical allurement. He heard Francis's canticle of creation resonating in Blake and Hopkins who sharpened his capacity to see the inscape and essential sanctity of creatures, as he later celebrated in one of his countless nature poems:

> For like a grain of fire
> smoldering in the heart of every living essence
> God plants His undivided power –
> Buries His though too vast for worlds

> In seed and roots and blade
> and flowers.[23]

Merton was learning to see that God shines not on creation but from within it, gently speaking in ten thousand things one divine wisdom. And it was such wisdom articulated by Catholic authors that led him to seek baptism in the Church, and soon after to ask admission to the Franciscan Order. But the Franciscans were not ready for Merton, and their refusal sent him to the Trappists whose hospitality was hospice for his wounded and disoriented soul.

When Merton arrived at the Abbey of Our Lady of Gethsemani in 1941 he was deeply contaminated by "the world" virus that had left him nearly crazy, in need of healing and recovery—in need of rebirth. He would later describe the soul-sickness he shared with his contemporaries to be an auto-immune disease of the spirit infecting the whole planet: "we destroy everything because we are destroying ourselves, spiritually, morally, in every way."[24] He sensed our violence to be symptomatic of a collective self-loathing, especially in the affluent world where we have numbed and drugged, with the artificial stuff of things, our deepest hungers for communion with creatures, the cosmos, and divinity. Once inside the monastic cloister, Merton found a safe haven in which to heal the deep afflictions of his alienated, fragmented soul. In this new environment of monastic silence and solitude, song and study, manual labor and meditation, Merton revived. He began to gather the self he had squandered in the disorienting ego-projects of his early life. Gethsemani felt like coming home to this wounded orphan man; it felt at last like the prodigal's reunion with the longed for Father, Adam's return to paradise. And the Earth itself—the beautiful expanse of the monastic enclosure—was powerful medicine for his anemic soul.

> I have not written what a paradise this place is, on purpose. I think it is more beautiful than any place I ever went to for its beauty—anyway it is the most beautiful place in America. I never saw anything like the country. A very wide valley—full of rolling and dipping land, woods, cedars, dark green fields—maybe young wheat. The monastery barns—vineyards ... And in the window comes the good smell of full fields.[25]

## Paradise mystic

In Gethsemani Merton learned that the quest for paradise was an explicitly Cistercian habit of heart, practiced in place by a vow of stability. The more his spirit settled in its new pastoral environment the easier it was to do the opening of soul and sensorium which Cistercian life invited. He was carried toward Eden by the rounds of daily prayer in choir, chanting hymns of the new creation with over a hundred monks who likewise were seeking paradise. In the company of "the innocent nations" of living beings he worked in the fields and the forest; they became his greater community, teaching him their sanity and simplicity. "Forest and field, sun and wind and sky, earth and water" all spoke the same silent language, reminding him that he had come to the monastery to develop like the things that grew all around him.[26] When Merton asked for greater solitude in the wilderness, his abbot named him forester, a job he relished because it allowed him to speak more freely and intimately with the sylvan world around him: "My brother and sister, the light and the water. The stump and the stone. The tables of rock. The blue, naked sky. Tractor tracks, a little waterfall ... solitude."[27] Eden was luring him on. The hermit bug had bitten him and he was swollen with the yearning for greater contemplative depth. Finally in 1965 he moved to a cinderblock cabin in the woods, a hermitage of his own where his practice of natural contemplation could deepen.

> There is no question for me that my one job as a monk is to live this hermit life in simple and direct contact with nature, primitively, quietly, doing some writing, maintaining such contacts as are willed by God and bearing witness to the value and goodness of simple things and ways, loving God in all of it. I am more convinced of this than of anything else in my life and I am sure it is what He asks of me.[28]

The hermitage became his re-birth chamber, and in the final years of life the labor pangs could be hard. He was sometimes infirm, lonely and at times depressed. He was conscious of living not just under the moon but under the bomb—SAC planes regularly skimmed the sky above his hermitage, so close that he could look up into the belly of the apocalyptic cherub and see its cargo. Yet he was in his Eden and he knew all the trees in his ecosphere, could name all the birds in his choir: "I know the birds in fact very well, for there are exactly fifteen pairs of birds living in the immediate area of my cabin and I share this particular place with them: we form an ecological balance."[29] There was a mental ecology too, a psychic commune of immortal poets, sages, philosophers, psalmists and prophets with whom he shared the deep vegetation of a forest more ancient than his: "…the deep forest in which the great birds Isaias and Jeremias sing. When I am most sickened by the things that are done by the country that surrounds this place I will take out the prophets and sing them in loud Latin across the hills and send their fiery words sailing south over the mountains to the place where they split atoms for the bombs in Tennessee."[30]

Merton's world also contained the non-ecology, "the destructive unbalance of nature, poisoned and unsettled by bombs, by fallout, by exploitation: the land ruined, the waters contaminated, the soil charged with chemicals, ravaged with machinery, the houses of farmers falling apart because everybody goes to the city and stays there …."[31] But Merton stayed in place, his vow of stability rooting him to his sylvan paradise. In some mysterious way he felt condemned to it, yet he could not have enough of the hours of silence when nothing happens: "When the clouds go by. When the trees say nothing."[32] But one tree ever spoke to him in silence: "the most beautiful of all the trees in the garden, at once the primordial paradise tree, the axis mundi, the cosmic axle, and the Cross.[33]

> I live in the woods out of necessity. I get out of bed in the middle of the night because it is imperative that I hear the silence of the night, alone, and, with my face on the floor, say psalms, alone, in the silence of the night. It is necessary for me to live here alone without a woman, for the silence of the forest is my bride and the sweet dark warmth of the whole world is my love, and out of the heart of that dark warmth comes the secret that is heard only in silence, but it is the root of all the secrets that are whispered by all the lovers in their beds all over the world ….[34]

Unexpectedly, in 1966, a woman did appear to breach the cloister of his heart and fill his woods with her presence. He had encountered her symbolically years before in premonitory waking and sleeping dreams. In her psychic form she was a young Jewess whom he called "Proverb"; when she visited poetically under the aspect of a nurse, he called her "Sophia."[35]

> Let us suppose that I am a man lying asleep in a hospital ... a soft voice awakens me from my dream. I am like all mankind awakening from all the dreams that ever were dreamed in all the nights of the world ... like the One Christ awakening in all the separate selves that ever were separate and isolated and alone in all the lands of the Earth ... into a unity of love. It is like the first morning of the world (when Adam, at the sweet voice of Wisdom awoke from nonentity and knew her), and like the Last Morning of the world when all the fragments of Adam will return from death at the voice of Hagia Sophia ... Such is the awakening of one man, one morning, at the voice of a nurse in a hospital. Awakening out of languor and darkness, out of helplessness, out of sleep, newly confronting reality and finding it to be gentleness. It is like being awakened by Eve ... in Paradise. In the cool hand of the nurse is the touch of all life, the touch of the Spirit.[36]

Two years before his death, Proverb, Sophia, Eve came to Merton incarnately. She was indeed a beautiful young student nurse assigned to care for him during his hospitalization for back surgery. Her own name was Margie. Merton was startled by the mysterious destiny of their encounter that offered him a rare experience of human communion. She became his sacrament of Eden, the beloved soul-mate he had never known before, and he celebrates their impossible relationship in paradisal metaphors throughout his *Midsummer's Journal*,[37] a collection of meditations written for her during their brief romance. But however redolent of paradise, their love was not to be consummated in this world, and Merton expressed the primacy of his espousal to the forest in a farewell letter to M.:

> Why do I live alone? I don't know ... it would be much more wonderful to be all tied up in someone ... and I know inexorably that this is not for me ... Freedom, darling. This is what the woods mean to me. I am free, free, a wild being, and that is all that I ever can

really be .... I am telling you: this life in the woods is IT. It is the only way. It is the way that everybody has lost ... it is life, this thing in the woods .... All I can say is that it is the life that has chosen itself for me.[38]

The two remaining years of Merton's life afforded an opportunity to travel to Alaska, California, and New Mexico in search of a new hermitage site that would allow deeper penetration into the sacred mysteries of the natural world. His joyous explorations of the numinous Earth accelerated his soul's journey into nature. Merton's paradise mind was expanding, and his journals from this period read like the geo-logues of an edenic poet.[39] "The new consciousness. Reading the calligraphy of snow and rock from the air. A sign of snow on a mountainside as if my own ancestors were hailing me. We bump. We burst into secrets."[40]

At last, in 1968, there was the journey to Asia, a lengthy pilgrimage that awakened him to the revelation of mountains as much as to the masters of the several Buddhist traditions he had gone to encounter. "O Tantric Mother Mountain! Yin Yang place of opposites in unity! ... The full beauty of the mountain is not seen until ... nothing more needs to be said ...."[41] Soon nothing more would be said; he was coming to his final illuminating station, wordless, empty, ready. He called it the most significant religious experience of his life, and, as it was in the beginning, it happened in a paradisal garden, the Buddhist cloister of Polonnaruwa, where trees, rocks, statues and sky all made evocations of Eden, just days before his death in Bangkok. On the other side of the world, Merton's paradise mind opened in "a beautiful and holy vision," tripped by a monumental image of the Buddha reclining in his deathless passing, radiating the truth of things: all is emptiness and compassion. "I don't know what else remains but I have now seen and have pierced through the surface and have got beyond the shadow and the disguise."[42] Within days of that edenic experience Merton was himself in the repose of deathless sleep, having solved the great mystery.

**Prophet of paradise**
The legacy that Merton leaves is not simply a rapturous poetics about creation but also a disturbing challenge to humankind's unconscionable

irresponsibly regarding our stewardship of even the most humble elements of Earth: "the life that moves without being seen and cannot be understood."[43] What the creation mystic celebrated in exquisite verse, the steely eco-prophet voiced with thunder: that the cause and the cure for Earth's degradation lay in the structures of human consciousness. He challenged us to come to our senses again, and cultivate the contemplative affluence that knows how useless it is "to look for what is everywhere," how "hopeless to hope for what cannot be gained because you already have it."[44]

Over fifty years ago Thomas Merton, the ecological prophet, knew what most of us are just waking up to: ours is a moment of supreme crisis presenting an almost incomprehensible emergency, and now, for the sake of planetary survival, ecological thinking has to become the hallmark of the new millennium.[45] Environmentalist Bill McKibbon calls our moment the end of nature;[46] geographer Jared Diamond calls it a civilizational collapse.[47] More ambivalently, geologian Thomas Berry calls it the end of the Cenozoic Age of planetary flourishing and the precipitous dawn of the Ecological Age when humankind, for the sake of survival, is challenged to learn a new mode of being on and with and as the Earth.[48] Our planet, our mother Gaia, which from her awesome beginnings has bountifully and mysteriously sustained the life of incalculable species, has been so violated and exhausted by her most recent offspring that her own survival is now in the hands of that youngest, reckless child.

While preparing this essay I spent a day in Merton's hermitage and found there *The Rule of Benedict*, patriarch of Western monasticism, which was the foundation of Merton's life as a Trappist monk. In reading again the manifesto of one of the great religious transformers of all time, I realized how formative that vision was for Merton, and how deeply he had imbibed and transmitted its restorative wisdom. Benedict offered not just a teaching of sane and wholesome human life within the greater biosphere, but possessed the genius and skill to encode it in a rule, incarnate it in a social body, fathering a family and a cultural tradition that in turn midwifed a new civilization. During his twenty-six year tenure under its suasion, Merton sensed himself to be a custodian and evolver of the Benedictine charism in Trappist form, reminding us that "in the night of our technological barbarism, monks must be as trees which exist silently in the dark and by their vital presence purify the air."[49]

A feature of Benedict's greatness is that he instinctively sensed the end of the world as he knew it, and he allowed that knowing to inform a radical response—a survival response in utopian form. He and his disciples imagined another way to construct a human society, other values, other configurations of just and non-violent life and development, a harmonious integration of the human within the great commune of creation, in light of the mystery of Christ and under the inspiration of the Gospel. One might argue that Benedict's world was not all that unlike our own, since we too are witnessing the collapse of a civilization built on our cherished and ubiquitously operative ideologies, and the technologies that underwrite them.

Benedict's apocalypse was the climax of a thousand year reign of Imperial Rome with its order, stability, complexity, and glorious achievements undone by spiritual and moral vacuity, its over extension, its militarization, its enslavement of weaker peoples and of the Earth itself; its oppression of both human and other-kind in its insatiable quest for power, pleasure, possession. Likewise, Merton and others would argue, we are suffering the climax of modern civilization—our petro-chemical age—and the technological and economic infrastructures that sustain it.[50] Our world-dream, under construction since the Enlightenment and fueled by the Industrial Revolution, peaked in the mid-twentieth century, just around the time Merton began his prophetic writing on the crises of our world. Built on both religious and secular millennial visions of unlimited progress, modernity was driven by materialist ideologies of human salvation and an uncritical faith in science and technology. And now, powered by a universally extractive economy, a triumphant capitalist ethos has wrapped the industrial/technological bubble around the globe, and at great cost in its progress.[51]

> There is no ... wretchedness so dismal as affluence. Wealth is poison. There is no misery to compare with that which exists where technology has been a total success. I know these are hard saying .... But do you imagine that if you become as prosperous as the United States you will no longer have needs? Here the needs are even greater. Full bellies have not brought peace and satisfaction

but dementia, and in any case not all the bellies are full either. But the dementia is the same for all.[52]

This modern *imperium* has required the carnage of countless beings to secure its hegemony over land, peoples, and resources. It has invented an arsenal of lethal weaponry capable of incinerating the whole planet. Although Merton did not have our statistical grids to map the dimensions of systemic destruction, he intuitively understood how our capitalist imperium has enslaved, impoverished or trafficked 70 percent of the human world, and left the whole biota—indeed even our geologic foundations—in trauma.

> The population of the affluent world is nourished on a steady diet of brutal mythology and hallucination, kept at a constant pitch of high tension by a life that is intrinsically violent in that it forces a large part of the population to an existence which is humanly intolerable ... the problem of violence then is ... the problem of a whole structure which is outwardly ordered and respectable, and inwardly ridden by psychopathic obsessions and delusions .... Violence today is white-collar violence, the systematically organized bureaucratic and technological destruction of man ... massively organized ... murder machine which threatens the world with destruction.[53]

As Rome fell from its classical form of hubris, we are falling by a modern variety all our own (as the current economic crisis portends). Even in the early 1960s Merton sensed the tectonic plates of unsustainable commerce and insatiable consumption dangerously shifting beneath us. He realized in horror that it was not just an empire falling, but the platform of creation itself, falling under the weight of our wants, our greed, our ignorance and arrogance, our waste, our need, our mechanization, our militarization, our exponentially increasing population that stands at the top of a food chain on the verge of depletion. Our planet, once the support of all life, now herself needs life-support, and for the most part, until this moment, the generational cohorts of modernity—particularly our captains of industry and government—have been clueless. Now we face ecocide and find ourselves bereft of even the moral and legal categories to address it.

If ever a world needed Merton's ecological wisdom and prophecy, it is ours: because half the world's tropical and temperate forests are now gone, half the wetlands, a third of the mangroves, twenty percent of the corals, ninety percent of the large predator fish, and seventy-five percent of the oceans are fished to capacity; because deforestation of the tropics continues at about an acre a second, and there are over two-hundred dead zones in the seas; because forty percent of U.S. fish species are threatened with extinction, a third of plants and amphibians, twenty percent of birds and mammals, and everywhere Earth's ice fields are melting; because species are disappearing a thousand times faster than ever. We are in an extinction spasm and the world of nature is disappearing by our own hand.[54]

> Almighty and merciful God, Father of all, Creator and Ruler of the Universe, Lord of History, whose designs are inscrutable, whose glory is without blemish, whose compassion is inexhaustible, in your will is our peace ... In this fatal moment of choice in which we might begin the patient architecture of peace [and sustainability] we may also take the last step across the rim of chaos. Save us then from our obsessions! Open our eyes, dissipate confusions, teach us to understand ourselves.[55]

**Eco-monasticism and eco-spirituality**

As Benedict and his disciples inspired the emergence of a new civilization by awakening and disciplining the spiritual energies of *his* generation, Merton believed that it is given to us to do the same for ours. Indeed, as Merton demonstrated time after time and taught the young monks in his care, the Benedictine ethos carries over with uncanny congruence to our own age with our need for the very vision, values and virtues Benedict proposed. Aware that in every generation, the human being must learn how to be "earthling" in Christian form, Benedict convened his first monastic school for the Lord's service, fashioning a holding environment for the rehabilitation and renewal of the human person. In this school, the highest merit goes to those who have mastered the creaturely way of humility, recovering their real status as members of the planetary community of living beings. His transformative curriculum of *lectio divina, ora et labora, conversatio morem, opus dei*,[56] a radical hospitality to all forms of life, and profound obedience to the voice of the Logos, was intended to cultivate the true self of the disciple. In such a school, as Merton the monk would discover, one's conscious center would in time become "the teeming heart of natural families."[57] For such education one is awarded no diploma: "one graduates by rising from the dead."[58]

The wisdom of Benedictine teaching and practice in our time of planetary crisis may be evolving into its most mature and necessary expression, and Merton remains its most prophetic interpreter. It holds out to the rest of the Christian community and the world at large, a model and method for reinventing the human being for an ecological age.[59] Its fundamental values and virtues, so eloquently elaborated by Merton, still beg embodiment: simplicity, frugality, fairness in distribution of resources, mindfulness in our habits of living. It is no coincidence, then, that the first pope of this new millennium should take Benedict for his namesake and patron. Modeling a response to the ecological mandates that spring from Saint Benedict's ecological values, the new Pope has reforested the Hungarian landscape with Vatican energy-offsets, rendering Catholic headquarters carbon neutral—the first nation state to do so. He has identified ecological sins for repentance in our disordered relation to creation, a list that could have been written by Merton.[60] Sounding many of Merton's themes, Benedict XVI's recent statements reiterate Benedict's call to blessed simplicity, to a sense of limits in order to transcend the anthrocentric egoism that is threatening the community of Earth by reducing everything to an object for human use, abuse, consumption, contamination, entertainment, adornment. Like Merton, the Pope also calls us to comprehend our environmental crisis as a spiritual crisis at root, and sets the practice of obedience on an ecological horizon: "obedience to the voice of the Earth," the most important voice for our future happiness.[61] "Existence itself, our Earth, speaks to us. We have to learn to listen," warns the Pope.[62] But Merton takes the work of obedience even further:

> Obedient unto death ... Perhaps the most crucial aspect of Christian obedience to God today concerns the responsibility of the Christian, in a technological society, toward ... God's creation and God's will for creation. Obedience to God's will for nature and

for man—respect for nature and love for man—in the awareness of our power to frustrate God's designs for nature and for man—to radically corrupt and destroy natural goods by misuse and blind exploitation, especially by criminal waste.[63]

Thomas Merton rehearsed his obedience to the voice of the Earth in conversation with countless dialogue partners. Three letters to women, in particular, offer insight into his prophetic sense of urgency regarding our ecological crisis. The first letter was written on January 12, 1963, to the mother of the environmental movement, Rachel Carson. He had just read her ground-shifting book, *Silent Spring*, her exposé of the catastrophic consequences of DDT use for pest control. Merton saw in this one instance the ubiquitous pathology of our technological civilization: the industrial-chemical assault on nature.

> The awful responsibility with which we scorn the smallest values is part of the same portentous irresponsibility with which we dare to use our titanic power in a way that threatens not only civilization but life itself. The same mental processing—I almost said mental illness—seems to be at work in both cases, and your book makes it clear to me that there is a consistent pattern running through everything we do, through every aspect of our culture, our thought, our economy, our whole way of life.[64]

Though Merton could not name this pathology explicitly, he insisted that the most urgent work of his moment was to diagnose its roots and try to find a cure for its cause. His own suspicion, echoed throughout his writings, was stark and stunning: "I would dare to say the sickness is perhaps a very real and very dreadful hatred of life as such, of course subconscious, buried under our pitiful and superficial optimism about ourselves and our affluent society."[65]

Because the dis-ease was at root a malady of soul, the healing therapy must address the soul: "The evil in the world is all our own making, and it proceeds entirely from our ruthless, senseless, wasteful, destructive, and suicidal neglect of our own being. This moral and spiritual disease is manifesting itself daily in symptoms that are more and more critical."[66]

"The neglect of being" is a familiar theme in Merton's work, the root cause of all our violence.[67] Failing to cultivate an inner affluence though contemplative living, we turn outward in an addictive pursuit of material affluence by embezzling the abundant planet. In order to survive in the style we want, we instinctively destroy everything on which our survival depends.[68] As with all addiction, the frustration of dissatisfied desire generates despair and a kind of self loathing. The awful fruit of that despair is an indiscriminate destructiveness. Beware says Merton: one cannot steal heaven or its vitality, as he often reminds us in his discourses on the pathos of Prometheus, the anxious thief of the primordial gift of existence itself.[69] Then Merton does what he will do in each of these three letters: he rehearses with Carson his understanding of the fall and original sin—an impulse to turn against life itself.[70] In every instance he reveals the depth of his life-long *lectio* of the Book of Genesis, and the consistency of his commentary in verdant themes of biophilic rapture and regret, awe and alarm. [71]

> The whole world itself ... has always appeared as a transparent manifestation of the love of God, as a "paradise" of His wisdom, manifested in all His creatures, down to the tiniest, and the most wonderful interrelationship between ....
> Man's vocation was to be in this cosmic creation, so to speak, as the eye of the body ... But man has lost his "sight" and is blundering about aimlessly in the midst of the wonderful works of God. It is in thinking that he sees, in gaining his power and technical know-how, that he has lost his wisdom and his cosmic perspective.[72]

Against the tapestry of the paradise tradition Merton laments our lost ability to read the scripture of nature and find our joy in it. He tells us that the duty of modern persons is to recover this ecological sight and insight, that we might see again the footprints of the Creator as signs of divine presence walking with us in the garden of Earth. Faithful to the spirit of Benedict, he tells Carson that it is the "vocation" of the modern person to unite our technics and wisdom in a supreme humility. Only humility can heal the hubris of the technologized psyche that perverts natural perspectives and denies our embeddedness in nature: "Denial of this only results in madness and cruelties."[73]

But can we recover, and how can we recover? The question, unanswered in 1963, is passed on to us, nearly a half-century later, nearly too late. And then, this postscript of hope: "A dangerous situation after all has certain spiritual advantages."[74]

The second letter, written nearly five years later, is a reply to Barbara Marx Hubbard, the nascent futurist scholar and founder of the Foundation for Conscious Evolution. Merton was one of a number of creative thinkers she invited to dialogue about how to awaken "the spiritual, social, and scientific potential of humanity, in harmony with nature for the highest good of all life."[75] Merton's response reveals his mounting sense of urgency regarding our planetary crisis: "There can be no question whatever that mankind now stands at one of the crucial thresholds of his existence. In some sense it is the most crucial, since the entire future is to a great extent in his own hands ... he can decide not just for himself ... but for the whole ... He can commit the future to a certain quality of life or no life at all."[76]

Now the human plays God with life in earnest. The edenic themes that ever fascinated Merton are writ large across a progressively ravaged earthscape. His hurried letters to Hubbard summarize much of his thinking: the roots of our crises lay in our structures of consciousness; the only way forward is in the reformation of human habits. *Conversatio morem* meets the noosphere as the moment by moment means of evolving human nature. Reaching toward hope once again he says salvation is still possible if we commit to new imperatives—a radical non-violence and non-exploitation of the living world. Biophilia is the only way forward—the recovery of our love and respect for life. Moreso, we must come into such intimacy with the life process that we instinctively, intuitively reverse the anxious habits of egoic self-survival with a trust "not in our own chances in a crap shoot," but in the inner dynamism of life itself.[77]

Perhaps most instructive are his final remarks to Hubbard distinguishing between the two conflicting mind-states of our post-modern cohort: millennial consciousness and ecological consciousness.[78] Millennial thinking sees the world as a provisional staging ground for some future religious, political or economic utopia arrived at by *metanoia*, conversion, or revolution. Its focus is human benefit, and in its secular forms is driven by Promethean hubris, a careless and stupid exploitation of the planet for short-term commercial, military, or technological ends which will be paid for by irreparable loss in living species and natural resources. But ecological thinking says this: "Look out! ... you run the risk of forgetting something. We are not alone in this thing. We belong to a community of living beings and we owe our fellow members in this community the respect and honor due to them. If we are to enter into a new era, well and good, but let's bring the rest of the living along with us."[79]

Merton closes his letter to Hubbard by invoking Albert Schweitzer and conservationist Aldo Leopold who give Merton language to summarize his understanding of ecological consciousness: a profound sense of the sacrality of all forms of life, requiring an ecological conscience to sustain it that expands the ethic of the Golden Rule. "A thing is right when it tends to preserve the integrity, stability and beauty of the biotic community. It is wrong when it tends otherwise."[80]

The last illuminating conversation is from Merton's correspondence with feminist theologian Rosemary Radford Ruether, also written in 1967. Though the volley of letters goes on for two years and covers many subjects in a range of emotional valences, most interesting are Merton's seminal thoughts on eco-monasticism. The letters between them are contentious. Ruether is leveling a fierce challenge to Merton's monastic choice as archaic, anomalous, institution bound, in service of its own mythology. The struggle for the realm of God is in the world, she insists, against the principalities and powers that hold it captive. In great detail the liberation theologian recounts for the Trappist hermit the creation-denying ethos and praxis of monasticism, its history of flight from the real world of conflict to the romantic refuge of nature. There is only one validating posture for contemporary monasticism, she insists: become a ministry to the world for the world. "If monasticism could view itself as a ministry, as a place to which the whole church could have recourse as a place of contemplation, but contemplation for the sake of the main arena of salvation which takes place precisely in the sphere of historical action, then it could take on a new relevance for modern persons."[81]

Merton's answer to her is immediate and visceral, sounding the fundamental ecological import of monastic structures and sensibility:

> ... monastic life is in closer contact with God's good creation and is simpler, saner more human than life in the supposedly pleasurable world. One of the things I love about my life ... is the fact that I live in the woods and according to a tempo of sun and moon and season in which it is naturally easy to walk in God's light ... through his creation. I seldom have to fuss with ... "recollecting myself" ... All you do is breathe and look around ....[82]

Merton reminds Ruether again of the root monastic charism: freedom from those very same powers and principalities that enslave the blind, disoriented millions who so destructively thrash about in an unrecognized paradise.[83] Hardly creation denying, it is the monastic person, entrained by the rhythms of the day and the round of the seasons, grounded by the vow of stability, who really knows the land which supports his or her existence. No, he says, monastics are the remnant of desperate conservationists. "You ought to know what hundreds of pine saplings I have planted myself and with the novices only to see them bulldozed by some ass a year later."[84]

In the late 1950s, tree planting and reforestation were not sentimental gestures in a region ravaged by coal and lumber companies. In fact Merton considered it a monastic responsibility to aid in reforesting the eroding woods. Could he ever have imagined what mountain top removal would do to the beloved bioregion which he had come to know so intimately and with which he lived so responsively? And on what front-line would this tree-hugging "hermit" position himself today in the devastating global wars of deforestation? One might hear him cheer the eco-monks of Thailand in their protective ordinations of vulnerable trees in the threatened forests of Asia.[85] Today these Buddhist monks play out more courageously and prophetically his own facetious offer to Rosemary Reuther forty years ago, that American monks should protect and administer our national forests.[86]

> In a word, to my mind the monk is one who not only saves the world in a theological sense, but saves it literally, protecting it

against the destructiveness of the rampaging city of greed, war ... And this loving care for natural creatures becomes in some sense, a warrant of (the monk's) theological mission and ministry as a (person) of contemplation.[87]

In defense of Merton, forty years on, let us acknowledge that he did in fact meet Ruether's challenge to make monasticism a ministry to the world. No other monk in history—save perhaps the Buddha—has had the extraordinary influence of Thomas Merton, the most well read monk of all time. His monastic ministry has been global in scope and perhaps more effective beyond the monastic world than within it. In the twentieth century, no other Christian master has awakened such hunger for prayer and prophetic practice, beginning with the report of his own soul quest, *The Seven Storey Mountain*. Since then, countless generations of his disciples have pursued the contemplative life in the anonymity of a virtual novitiate under his direction, their *lectio*, Merton's enormous library of spiritual wisdom written in a contemporary idiom, which proscribes a contemplative curriculum for the recovery of paradise mind: "living the life of the new creation in which right relation to all the rest of God's creatures is fully restored."[88]

In Merton's vision, the theological mission of these worldly contemplatives interfaces with an ecological mission: to embody a mode of Christian life that can restore the human person in Christ, to our original state, conscious of paradise all around. In this broader appeal we hear him say that it is "the job of the worldly contemplative" to render iconoclastic criticism of the religion of human progress and planetary hegemony. It is "the job of the worldly contemplative" to embody Edenic sanity and cultivate gardens of paradise at the heart of the Church for the sake of the world. It is "the job of worldly contemplatives" to become an Edenic cohort again, a new race of Christic beings who in this night of our technological barbarism, are as trees "which ... by their vital presence purify the air."[89]

> It is not easy to try and say what I know I cannot say ... The reality that is present to us and in us: Call it Being, call it Atman, call it Pneuma ... or Silence. And the simple fact that by being attentive, by learning to listen (or recovering the natural capacity to

listen which cannot be learned any more than breathing), we can find ourselves engulfed in such happiness that it cannot be explained: the happiness of being at one with everything that is hidden in the ground of Love for which there can be no explanations. I suppose what makes me most glad is that we recognize each other in this metaphysical space of silence and happiness, and get some sense, for a moment, that we are "full of paradise without knowing it."[90]

## Notes

1. Merton, Thomas, "'Baptism in the Forest': Wisdom and Initiation in William Faulkner," in *The Literary Essays of Thomas Merton*, ed. Brother Patrick Hart (New York: New Directions, 1981), p. 108.
2. Merton, Thomas, *Conjectures of a Guilty Bystander* (Garden City, NY: Doubleday, 1966), p. 132.
3. Merton, Thomas, "Baptism in the Forest," p. 108.
4. Merton, Thomas, "The General Dance," in *New Seeds of Contemplation* (New York: New Directions, 1962), p. 290.
5. Merton, Thomas, "The General Dance," pp. 290-91.
6. Merton, Thomas, "Theology of Creativity," in *The Literary Essays of Thomas Merton*, ed. Brother Patrick Hart (New York: New Directions, 1981), p. 368.
7. Merton, Thomas, "Theology of Creativity," p. 368.
8. Merton, Thomas, *A Search for Solitude: The Journals of Thomas Merton* Vol. 3, ed. Lawrence Cunningham (San Francisco: Harper San Francisco, 1966), pp. 189-90.
9. In this, Merton reiterates the insights of Teilhard de Chardin and Thomas Berry who perceive the human as the emergent consciousness of the evolutionary process of creation, the Earth's way of understanding itself.
10. Merton, Thomas, *New Seeds of Contemplation* (New York: New Directions, 1962), p. 5.
11. Merton, Thomas, "Hagia Sophia," in *The Collected Poems of Thomas Merton* (New York: New Directions, 1977), p. 363.
12. Merton, Thomas, "Hagia Sophia," p. 363.
13. Merton, Thomas, "Theology of Creativity," p. 369.
14. Merton, Thomas, "Theology of Creativity," pp. 355 ff.
15. Merton, Thomas, "Baptism in the Forest," p. 108.
16. See Merton, Thomas, "Prometheus: A Meditation," in *A Thomas Merton Reader*, ed. Thomas McDonnell (Garden City, NY: Image Books, 1974).
17. Merton, Thomas, "The Early Legend," in *The Collected Poems of Thomas Merton*, pp. 757-8.
18. "Tom's Book," an unpublished journal by Ruth Jenkins Merton. See *The Merton Encyclopedia*, ed. William H. Shannon, Christine M. Bochen, Patrick O'Connell (Maryknoll, NY: Orbis, 2002), p. 489.
19. Merton, Thomas, *The Sign of Jonas* (New York: Harcourt, Brace and Co.,1953), p. 253.

20. Merton, Thomas, *The Seven Storey Mountain*, p. 11.
21. Merton, Thomas, "From Pilgrimage to Crusade," in *Mystics and Zen Masters* (New York: Farrar, Straus and Giroux), p. 97.
22. Merton, Thomas, "From Pilgrimage to Crusade," p. 97.
23. Merton, Thomas, "The Sowing of Meanings" in *The Collected Poems of Thomas Merton*, p. 187.
24. Merton, Thomas, *Turning Toward the World: The Journals of Thomas Merton* Vol. 4, ed. Victor Kramer (San Francisco: Harper San Francisco, 1996), p. 274.
25. Merton, Thomas, *Run to the Mountain: The Journals of Thomas Merton* Vol. 1, ed. Patrick Hart, OSCO (San Francisco: Harper San Francisco, 1995), p. 347.
26. Merton, Thomas, *The Waters of Siloe* (New York: Harcourt Brace, 1949), pp. 273-74.
27. Merton, Thomas, *Entering the Silence: The Journals of Thomas Merton* Vol. 2, ed. Jonathan Montaldo (San Francisco: Harper San Francisco, 1996), p. 412.
28. Merton, Thomas, *Dancing in the Water of Life: The Journals of Thomas Merton* Vol. 5, ed. Robert Daggy (San Francisco: Harper San Francisco, 1996), p. 229.
29. Merton, Thomas, *Dancing in the Water of Life*, p. 239.
30. Merton, Thomas, *Dancing in the Water of Life*, p. 240.
31. Merton, Thomas, *Dancing in the Water of Life*, p. 240.
32. Merton, Thomas, "*A Midsummer Diary for M.*" in *Learning to Love: The Journals of Thomas Merton* Vol. 6, ed. Christine Bochen (San Francisco: Harper San Francisco, 1997), p. 341.
33. Merton, Thomas, *Dancing in the Water of Life*, p. 240.
34. Merton, Thomas, *Dancing in the Water of Life*, p. 240.
35. For a synopsis of Merton's mystical relationship to "Proverb" and "Sophia" see *The Thomas Merton Encyclopedia*, pp. 374-45; 191-93.
36. Merton, Thomas, "Hagia Sophia," p. 363.
37. Merton, Thomas, "*A Midsummer Diary for M.*," pp. 301-48.
38. Merton, Thomas, "*A Midsummer Diary for M.*," p. 342.
39. See "The Edenic Office of the Poet," *The Literary Essays of Thomas Merton*, p. 29.
40. Merton, Thomas, *The Other Side of the Mountain: The Journals of Thomas Merton* Vol. 7, ed. Patrick Hart, OSCO (San Francisco: Harper San Francisco, 1997), p. 94.
41. Merton, Thomas, *The Other Side of the Mountain*, p. 286.
42. Merton, Thomas, *The Asian Journal of Thomas Merton,* ed. Naomi Burton Stone, James Laughlin, Patrick Hart, OSCO (New York: New Directions, 1973), p. 236.
43. Merton, Thomas, "Atlas and the Fat Man" in *The Collected Poems of Thomas Merton*, p. 691.
44. Merton, Thomas, "Atlas and the Fat Man," p. 691.
45. See below Merton's correspondence with Rachel Carson, in Thomas Merton, *Witness to Freedom: Letters in Time of Crisis*, selected and edited by William H. Shannon (New York: Farrar, Straus, Giroux, 1994), p. 70 ff.
46. McKibbon, Bill, *The End of Nature* (New York: Random House Publishing Group, 2006).
47. Diamond, Jared, *Collapse: How Civilizations Choose to Fail or Succeed* (New York: Viking Adult, 2004).
48. Berry, Thomas, *The Great Work: Our Way into the Future* (New York: Bell Tower, 1999).

49. Merton, Thomas, *The Monastic Journey*, (Kansas City: Sheed Andrews and McMeel, 1977), p. 38.
50. See Berry, Thomas, "The Extractive Economy," and "The Petroleum Interval," in *The Great Work*, pp. 136-66.
51. For a comprehensive analysis of the progress of "the age of human devastation," see Thomas Berry's *The Great Work*.
52. Merton, Thomas, *Dancing in the Water of Life*, p. 240.
53. Merton, Thomas, "Toward a Theology of Resistance," in *Faith and Violence: Christian Teaching and Christian Practice* (Notre Dame, IN: University of Notre Dame Press, 1968), p. 3.
54. Litany created from statistics in Speth, Gustav, *The Bridge at the Edge of the World: Capitalism, the Environment, and Crossing from Crisis to Sustainability* (Yale Press, 2008).
55. Merton, Thomas, *Passion for Peace*, ed. William Shannon (New York: Crossroad Publishing Company, 1997), pp. 327-29.
56. *Lectio divina, ora et labora, conversatio morem, opus dei*, comprise the spiritual structure of the Benedictine life. *Lectio divina* is the daily practice of reading the sacred scriptures; *ora et labora* are the pillars of Benedictine life composed in prayer and work; *conversatio morem* is the root vow of the monk, a commitment to a life-long transformation of one's habits of life; and *opus dei* the primary work of the monk—the ceaseless sung praise of God in the liturgy of the hours prayed in choir with the community.
57. "Cables to the Ace," *The Collected Poems of Thomas Merton* (New York: New Dimensions, 1977), p. 443.
58. Merton, Thomas, *Love and Living*, ed. Naomi Burton Stone and Patrick Hart (New York: Bantam Edition, 1980), p. 4.
59. This is the fundamental theme of Thomas Berry's *The Great Work*.
60. Bishop Gianfranco Girotti, Regent of the Penitentiary in *L'Oservatore Romano* March, 2008 spoke of new forms of social sin: genetic manipulation, environmental pollution, social inequality, excessive wealth.
61. Benedict XVI, quoted in "For Benedict Environmental Movement Promises Recovery of Natural Law Tradition, by John Allen. The National Catholic Reporter, "All Things Catholic," Friday July 27, 2007, Vd. 6, No 47. (http://ncrcafe.org/node/1241).
62. Pope Benedict XVI.
63. Merton, Thomas, *The Journals of Thomas Merton* Vol. 5, ed. Robert Daggy, *Dancing in the Water of Life* (San Francisco: Harper San Francisco, 1997), p. 227.
64. Merton, Thomas, *Witness to Freedom: Letters in Time of Crisis*, selected and edited by William H. Shannon (New York: Farrar, Straus, Giroux, 1994), p. 70.
65. Merton, Thomas, *Witness to Freedom: Letters in Time of Crisis*, p. 71.
66. Merton, Thomas, *Conjectures of a Guilty Bystander*, p. 222.
67. See Deignan, Kathleen, CND, "Thomas Merton: Soul of the Age," in *Monastic Interreligious Dialogue Bulletin* 74, April 2005.
68. Merton, Thomas, *Conjectures of a Guilty Bystander*, p. 222.
69. Merton, Thomas, "Promethean Theology," in *The New Man* (New York: Mentor-Omega Book, 1961), pp. 21-35.
70. Merton, Thomas, *Witness to Freedom*, p. 70.

71. For a consideration of Merton's creation centered spirituality see Merton, Thomas, *When the Trees Say Nothing—Writings on Nature,* ed. Kathleen Deignan, CND (Notre Dame, IN: Sorin Books, 2003). See also Monica Weis, Patrick O'Connell, and Paul Pearson for their work on Merton's ecological consciousness, nature poetry, and sense of place.
72. Merton, Thomas, *Witness to Freedom,* p. 70.
73. Merton, Thomas, *Conjectures of a Guilty Bystander,* pp. 294-95.
74. Merton, Thomas, *Witness to Freedom,* p. 72.
75. See Barbara Marx Hubbard's website: http://www.evolve.org/pub/doc/footer_about_fce.html
76. Merton, Thomas, *Witness to Freedom,* pp. 72-73.
77. Merton, Thomas, *Witness to Freedom,* p. 73.
78. Merton, Thomas, *Witness to Freedom,* pp. 74-75.
79. Merton, Thomas, *Witness to Freedom,* p. 74.
80. Merton, Thomas, *Witness to Freedom,* p. 74, quoting Aldo Leopold.
81. *At Home in the World: The Letters of Thomas Merton and Rosemary Radford Ruether,* Mary Tardiff, OP, ed. (Maryknoll, New York: Orbis Books, 1995), p. 30.
82. *At Home in the World,* pp. 34-5.
83. *At Home in the World,* p. 31.
84. *At Home in the World,* p. 35.
85. See http://environment.harvard.edu/religion/religion/buddhism/projects/thai_ecology.html.
86. *At Home in the World,* p. 35.
87. *At Home in the World,* p. 35.
88. *At Home in the World,* pp. 35-36.
89. Merton, Thomas, *The Monastic Journey,* p. 38.
90. *The Hidden Ground of Love: The Letters of Thomas Merton on Religious Experience,* ed. William Shannon (New York: Farrar, Straus, Giroux, 1985), p. 115.

# THOMAS MERTON'S RE-VISIONING THE NEW WORLD AT INTERCULTURAL BORDERS

Malgorzata Poks

Much has been written about Merton's 1958 illuminative experience in downtown Louisville, when he suddenly experienced himself strongly united to the whole of the human race and rejoiced in the secret beauty of every person's heart. But not many Merton readers realize that this breakthrough moment was in fact a culmination of a long process and that adopting American citizenship was an earlier step toward an awareness of that larger, transcultural identity.[1] This may come as a surprise to anyone familiar with Merton's critique of American international and domestic policy. In the last decade of his life he did not spare the United States harsh words, calling it a police state; a mad, totalitarian country; a country under judgment; "a swinish culture";[2] "one of the most decadent societies on the face of the earth."[3] He repeatedly accused his adopted country of genocide; of a corrupting love of wealth and power; moral and spiritual blindness. The America of his day appeared to be an epitome of the most explosive of western myths: that of *Civitas Christiana*, a Christian civilization, which had often served as a mere excuse for exploiting, enslaving, destroying, and inflicting untold suffering on numerous non-Christian cultures. Given this context, it might sound strange that Merton thought highly of his own American destiny and even adopted the rhetoric of "the Great Vocation of America."[4]

The idea of the United States' divinely ordered Manifest Destiny, used to justify the country's sometimes reckless westward expansion while downplaying the venture's enormous human and environmental cost, acquired in the twentieth century additional, equally if not more sinister, connotations. For one thing, with the geographical frontier closed, it was outer space that now seemed to offer possibilities of almost endless expansion and exploitation, for both commercial and military purposes. For another, at the height of the Cold War, this powerful country that had already used the atomic bomb on a "civilian target" assumed the role of the guardian of democracy and was mounting a world-wide anti-Communist crusade which was to engage its military forces practically all over the world. Favoring the Big Stick policy, the United States was often perceived abroad as "A wealthy country,/joining the cult of Mammon to the cult of Hercules;/while Liberty, lighting the path/to easy conquest, raises her torch in New York."[5] The critical racial situation within the country completing the picture, one may wonder what "great" vocation Merton was thinking about in mid twentieth-century and, if he could nonetheless resort to the apparently discredited "chosen land" rhetoric, could we perhaps learn from him to remain hopeful about it despite appearances to the contrary?

This article will argue that Merton's desire to help America to realize its "marvelous" destiny articulates the spiritual consciousness of a New World that has not yet been born. This is an integrated, all-inclusive consciousness of the new man and woman, a consciousness that accepts the Doppelgänger in itself and thus has the capability to heal the intracultural split.[6] In this context it should come as no surprise that Merton's understanding of America was undergoing revisions, redefinitions and a steady broadening of perspectives, until it became synonymous with a truly *new* reality: the realized eschatology of the Kingdom that is still coming and, at the same time, has always been "kenotically" present in the confusion of history. Merton never made this equation (between America and the "new" world) explicit, yet this reading seems entirely legitimate. Additionally, in the process of negotiating the oppositional and antagonistic elements within his "American" identity, Merton could hardly avoid critiquing the simplistic essentialist position of traditional notions of identity. In consequence of a series of literal and metaphorical encounters with "other Americans," through border-crossings and self-translations, he was instinctively moving toward the more ambiguous understanding of identity as politics rather than simply inheritance, as roots *as well as* routes. In *Travel and Translation*, a book written "at the end of what will surely be the last 'Western' millennium," James Clifford worries about the ways of "navigat[ing] the repressive alternatives of universalism and separatism."[7] Clifford argues that recovering the history of "traveling East," as a counterproposition to the broadly construed cultural experience of "traveling West," might prove of crucial importance. My argument is that Merton's American re-visions provide ample glimpses of such a venture.

### American citizenship as a spiritual question

On the eve of World War II, just before entering the Abbey of Gethsemani, Merton wrote a semi-autobiographical novel he provisionally entitled *Journal of My Escape from the Nazis* (published in 1969 as *My Argument with the Gestapo*). In response to questions about his nationality, the novel's protagonist refuses to identify himself with any country, assumes the stance of an "innocent bystander," a free and independent human being who represents only himself. But what seemed to be an act of courage and a gesture of dissent, ten years later looked more like "the confession of [Merton's] own nonentity."[8] Having been a Gethsemani monk for nine years, Merton was beginning to realize that his spiritual detachment from the proud and confused world could not be an end in itself, but rather a means of reassessing and reestablishing his relation with it. In 1951 it suddenly dawns on him that citizenship is "a question of justice and charity," that America "is worth loving," and that everyone living in a given place is shaped by it and therefore indebted to it.[9] Withdrawing from a troubled world and protesting one's imagined innocence was no longer a solution, but sheer illusion and irresponsibility. Merton's long immersion in contemplative silence and his studies in Cistercian spirituality prepared him for the recognition that the world made by God is still basically good and that a follower of Christ must try to redeem it, instead of condemning it. "The sanity of St. Benedict has something to do with the mystery of a monk becoming an American citizen,"[10] he speculates, ready to accept himself as he is, "Gethsemani as it is, America as it is—atomic bomb and all."[11] When several months later Merton signs his naturalization papers (June 1951), he does this with full consciousness that he really belongs both to the racially segregated American South and to the country at large; that the failings of America are also his own; and that his destiny is bound with the place God has chosen for him. "Perhaps," he speculates later in the pages of *The Sign of Jonas*, "I am called upon to objectify the truth that America, for all its evil, is innocent and somehow ignorantly holy."[12] Evidently, already concerned with the dialectic of true and false self, Merton was hoping to reach the country's true self, its *point vierge*, and thus help America become what is was meant to be: a *New* World, a land of promise.

Merton's desire was all the more pressing in the context of his realization that he could enter deeper into solitude only by bearing the burdens of those entrusted to him and leaving his own burdens to others. He was thinking specifically about his scholastics, but all his other neighbors (in the biblical sense of the word), would qualify as well. "What is my new desert?" he asks in November 1951. "The name of it is *compassion*."[13] Next he declares: "I die of love for you, Compassion: I take you for my Lady, as Francis married poverty, I marry you, the Queen of hermits and the Mother of the poor."[14] This symbolic marriage to Lady Compassion was, obviously, a defining moment in his life. From now on, he dedicates himself to the defense of what is poorest and humblest in the world at large and in every human being, no matter how self-righteous they may seem to be. Parenthetically speaking, this gesture also dimly foreshadows the master theme of Merton's later life: his search for and dedication to Sophia, the feminine aspect of God and another manifestation of Lady Compassion.

Clearly, the Merton of Compassion had no choice but engage in some spiritual and mystical action that would ally him with the blessed of the Sermon on the Mount wherever they might be. Theoretically, the monastic life is one of poverty, humility, simplicity. But living in a busy modern monastery, Merton realized how little poverty is really understood in the western world (especially in his highly developed America) and how secure the life of Gethsemani monks really is. Solidarity with the poor requires sacrifice, a refusal to be part of a prosperous and exploitative society, a break with "the collective sin of American society and American Catholicism."[15] This reflection was prompted by Merton's meditation on original sin as contracted from the *collective* Adam, i.e., from society. The original sin of the collective American Adam that Merton is part of made for stagnation in his prayer life: "How offer to God prayer as an act of justice if I am living in injustice?" he thunders. The only solution he can find is this: by abandoning that exterior, "tribal" society and seeking to create "a spiritual community which transcends national, social, and especially tribal limitations."[16] On the one hand, this observation seems to imply that beyond the "fallen," exterior American self, there is an inner self which, when accessed, can serve as a basis for constructing a transnational spiritual community; on the other, Merton frequently despairs of this "other" America and denounces the country wholesale. There is no doubt that his attitude to the United States was an indicator of the tensions and ambiguities he felt about his membership in those other communities: the monastery of Our Lady of Gethsemani; the Cistercian Order; the Roman Catholic Church; last but not least, the human race itself. By the 1960s, the time of his most creative engagement with existentialism, Merton becomes—intellectually and emotionally—more reconciled to the truth that fleeing the collective sin of his society (whether broadly of narrowly understood) is no way to construct a spiritual community: since we are members one of another, we will either be saved together or lost together. The spiritual community will come about only by working through the collective sin, so that the very Adam that has sinned would be redeemed.

But in the 1950s Merton was still hoping for a more unambiguous, perhaps more spectacular alliance. "The people of God," he claimed, "are the poor of the world, in Africa, Asia, Latin America."[17] In 1958 Merton asks a sculptor from Ecuador, Jaime Andrade, for a statue of a Black Virgin with Child for the Novitiate. "A statue," as he explains, "that would tell the truth about God being 'born' Incarnate in the Indians of the Andes. Christ poor and despised among the disinherited of the earth."[18] Although in pre-Gethsemani days he had already recognized God's favorite children among the people of color within his own society (one example is his attraction to Harlem's poor and the subsequent work with Catherine de Hueck), now he was more predisposed to recognize God's elect outside national borders. It was the indigenous population of the economically underdeveloped, yet spiritually rich areas of the hemisphere that became especially close to his heart. More interestingly perhaps, it was his deep understanding of, and a heartfelt compassion for, the plight of the Latin American "other" that in time re-turned Merton to the Afro-American and the North American Indian as well, and that was to launch him toward additional social and cultural criticism.

**Glimpse of the true America**

Not surprisingly, when the idea of Merton's American destiny resurfaces, it is the entire hemisphere he has in mind. In February 1958, having already been exposed to Latin American issues through his contacts with the Nicaraguan novice at Gethsemani, Ernesto Cardenal, and the possibility of helping to found a Cistercian foundation in Ecuador, Merton suddenly experiences one of those moments "when many unrelated pieces of one's life fall into place in a great unity towards which one has been growing."[19] The language of epiphany is not accidental: what now seems to be giving unity to the monk's life is his calling to "be oneself a whole hemisphere and help the hemisphere to realize its own destiny."[20] But the True America he envisions is a continent still in need of discovery.[21] Merton understands that the North is incomplete without the South and vice versa, and that both continents have something precious to offer to each other. Striving toward a holistic perspective and aspiring to be himself a man of the whole hemisphere, he wants to work toward a new consciousness that does not erase difference but embraces it and integrates "all the extremes [...] without eclecticism, without dilettantism, without false mysticism, without being torn apart."[22]

The work of reclamation and integration is vital, since what generally passes for "American culture," and is imitated all over the world as such, is often the result of the *rejection* of roots, an ignorance of the continent's heritage, and this results in America becoming "a sort of cancerous orchid transplanted from somewhere else."[23] Merton's dream of helping the true, free and spiritual America to come finally to maturity demands, therefore, an enormous intellectual effort to reclaim the hemisphere's multiple roots, an effort to integrate for Merton in himself the cultural influences of colonial England, Spain, and Portugal, along with the "deeper roots"[24] of the Indian. If needs be, it also demands that he *become* the "other" so as to bring this other—the poor Indian *campesino*, the oppressed, the suffering, the underprivileged—into the cultural orbit of the developed, predominantly white, middle-class America—whether North or South.

Soon Merton was to read voraciously and write voluminously to and about Latin Americans, treating his growing expertise as reparation for the ignorance, as well as arrogance, of his countrymen and women. Once again he expresses growing unease about his U.S. citizenship. Clearly, the full acceptance of his North American identity was more problematic than he had imagined. In mid-1959 Merton records his inner struggle. Swinging from one extreme to the other, he writes about

> The responsibility before God to separate myself from a civilization that is utterly contemptible and false and heading for its own destruction. (Read about the atomic submarines that can fire an ICBM with an atomic warhead from under 1,000 miles from "target." Target being of course an open city with millions of innocent and defenseless people in it. This is utterly beyond bearing.). But here at Geth[semani] I am a kind of spiritual spokesman and a figurehead for such a society. Before God I have an obligation to leave the society as best I can.[25]

**Sophia**

It is symptomatic that Merton should finally see Latin America in sophianic terms. In 1958, in the preface to the Argentine edition of his *Complete Works* (of which only one volume appeared) he dares to hope that her silent, feminine voice would awaken the "grand, powerful, rich, intelligent" North (whose audacity is nonetheless counterbalanced by "a surprising humility"[26]) to its larger hemispheric vocation of identity in complementarity. Figuratively feminized, in contradistinction to the strong, Promethean North, it was the land where the sweet and merciful voice of Hagia Sophia, coming to awaken all humankind from the dream of separateness, would not be drowned in the noise of activism and the eloquence of atomic explosions. Steeped in readings in sophianic theology (Nicolai Berdyaev, Macarius Bulgakov, Paul Evdokimov) and by a powerful grip of his recurrent Proverb dreams, Merton mourned the fact that the feminine aspect of God: that of love, mercy, compassion, tenderness, humility, and hiddenness, was largely obscured in the modern world which was overtly masculine, patriarchal, and ruthlessly dedicated to a pursuit of power. Since "all reality mirrors the reality of God," Merton wrote in a letter to his artist-friend Victor Hammer, "the 'masculine-feminine' relationship is basic in *all* reality."[27] Trying to counterbalance the official North American rituals of power by retrieving and revaluing the feminine was, therefore, part of Merton's mission to help the new, integrated America he imagined to come into being. "Sophia," he continues in the same letter, "is the feminine, dark, yielding, tender counterpart of the power, justice, creative dynamism of the Father."[28] In the same way, the Indian and Hispanic South appeared to him as a necessary counterpart of the rich, largely Protestant and Anglo-Saxon North.

It is significant to remember, however, that this North–South relationship is contextualized as part of an overall masculine-feminine dynamics characteristic of every aspect of reality. And so, in his 1963 poetic vision, the prose-poem "Hagia Sophia," Merton would identify Divine Wisdom, "the "mysterious Unity and Integrity," with "the child who is prisoner in *all* the people, and who says nothing."[29] Being one with Her demanded solidarity not only with the silenced victims of oppression, including that caused by North American consumerism and political supremacy, but perhaps more demandingly, with every, however ruthless, person's *repressed inner* child—that point of absolute incorruptibility, which is God's own image in everyone. This realization opens Merton's broader American identity to an all-inclusive reading, and one he would undoubtedly endorse: after 9/11 solidarity with the suddenly vulnerable United States was instantaneous; people of good will bound together in a transnational, transcultural realization that we all had been attacked; that, in consequence, "we are all Americans." Briefly after 9/11 the veil of spurious audacity was lifted, revealing another America, the one which Merton had been intuiting all along: surprisingly humble and somehow innocently holy. In the silence that followed, Hagia Sophia could whisper words of compassion and solace to the victims of fear wherever they were and however self-assured they had appeared the day before.

### The inner American "I"

As already suggested, the beginning of Merton's fascination with and growing expertise in Hispanic America is to be traced to the project of establishing an American Cistercian foundation south of the border. His near fluency in the Spanish language seemed to predispose Merton to be part of that venture. He took to the idea as fish to water. In July 1957 Merton considered the possibility in somewhat romantic terms: what he envisions is a poor contemplative community living the life of prayer and solidarity with impoverished Indians as reparation for the white world's sins: "our [North American] sins and the sins of all conquerors, particularly, of the conquistadores."[30] At the end of August that year he speculates about the various alternatives, considering the pluses and minuses of each: the island of Ometepe in Nicaragua; the environs of Medellin or the Cauca Valley in Colombia; Venezuela—almost limitless possibilities; Paraguay. His emotions soar: "I am fascinated," "I weep to think of it."[31] The community could grow coffee, sugar cane, oranges, and lemons; they would set up a clinic; organize reunions of intellectuals; live the spiritual life of truth, justice, and humility and; generally, be "on the side of progress and social justice"[32] where usually the hierarchical Church traditionally allies herself with tyranny and power. At other times Merton dreams of living the life of a hermit on an Indian reservation. Perhaps the first sobering moment comes with a letter from Jaime Andrade, who cautions Merton that once in the South, he would be inevitably caught between the reactionary ruling and ecclesiastical elites on the one hand, and the communist intelligentsia on the other, hampered and antagonized by both.[33] But in the fifties he was still largely ignorant of the real complexities of Latin American politics.

Much was to be learned in this respect from the recently admitted novice from Nicaragua, Ernesto Cardenal (1925-), who was to leave the monastery only two years later (1959) due to health problems. Prior to entering Gethsemani, Cardenal had taken part in an armed conspiracy against the elder Somosa and written poetry with political content. Now Cardenal was introducing his Novice Master to Latin American reality, sharing with him his fascination with Maya Indians, and putting Merton in touch with a range of poets and intellectuals from the Latin countries. One of the earliest contacts was Cardenal's cousin, Pablo Antiono Cuadra, publisher and poet working in the indigenist tradition, leader of a literary movement *la Vanguardia*. His "Notes On How to Reach the Inner Indian," one of the *Vanguardists*' key manifestos, specified that after modernism's discovery of the Indian as a picturesque stranger, the discovery and acceptance of the inner Indian, the intimate Indian, the other American "I," was now necessary.[34] This is an important point: the Indian as the other American "I" is obviously a sort of Jungian anima for the hemisphere, the feminine part of the double continent's masculine self, its gender opposite soul that needs to be acknowledged and embraced. Since this anima is a more oriental than occidental concept,[35] the fully integrated western hemisphere would have to reclaim its long-forgotten Eastern roots. Merton was fully conscious of this fact. Deeply impressed by Cuarda's collection of verse entitled *El jaguar y la luna*, he tellingly praises it as "at once very Asiatic and very American," and "the voice of the true America."[36]

One of the poems in that collection, "The Secret of the Burning Stars," moved Merton strongly. It presents a dialogue between two stars. Merton explains: "Indians believed that warriors and mothers became 'stars' in heaven because of their suffering." Then he adds: "The warrior says he died that the future might be born and that he has not seen that future. This was what most moved me, because perhaps this is also my own destiny."[37] A telling comment. Unlike Moses, he might not even be allowed a glimpse of the spiritual America he is striving to bring forth. But, as Merton well knew, a genuine monk should not attach himself to results; his task was to witness to truth regardless of consequences and trust that the truth would take care of itself.

Just a few days before meeting Cuadra, in April 1958, Merton had been reading John Collier's revisionist book *The Indians of the Americas* and felt ashamed at being part of a society that, under the pretext of bringing Christ to the world, actually "killed the Innocents," forced the entire world to worship its own image, and exiled Christ to a new land of captivity. Or rather Christ himself chose exile and solidarity with the crucified part of humanity. The sense of shame and shared responsibility for conquest, colonization, and extermination of Native Americans is devastating. "Have we ever yet become Christians?" Merton ponders in his journal.[38] Soon he would be openly denouncing the West for its reckless treatment of indigenous peoples, as well as for its failure to listen to the prophetic wisdom of Indian America's lost civilizations. "Did anyone pay attention to the voices of the Maya and the Inca who had deep things to say?"[39] he was to ask in 1961 in an open letter "Concerning Giants" addressed to Cuadra and intended as "a statement of where I stand, morally, as a Christian writer."[40] Living in the country of Magog but critical of its policies, Merton decided to dedicate his life to listening and sensitizing the conscience of his compatriots to the providential and prophetic messages so often detectable in the voice of the "stranger" whom the proud world continued to ignore. Merton's ministry of listening can be seen as a vital part of his effort to reclaim a neglected or forgotten part of America's collective identity.

**A ministry of listening**

Conscious that his first duty was to listen to and learn from the poorest and humblest peoples, that is, the American Indians, already in 1958 Merton began a serious study of pre-Conquest history, the art of ancient Mesoamerica, and recent publications by and about Indians. With Ernesto Cardenal Merton discussed Black Elk's *The Sacred Pipe*, read with interest the indigenist poetry and other materials sent by Cuadra, and steeped himself in the *Chilam Balam* holy writings. To a growing number of his Latin American contacts he would confide the urgent need, bordering on a sense of mission, to hear the voice of the new man rooted in the American soil and waiting to be born. In a letter to Ernesto Cardenal, dated July 12, 1964, he insists on the obligation to "listen to the silence of the Indian" and hear at last "all that has not been said for five hundred years. The salvation of our lives depends on it."[41] The following detailed explanation of this apparently exaggerated claim says much about Merton's own sense of calling, and therefore merits being quoted at length. Praising Cardenal for his texts about San Blas Indians, Merton assures his former novice:

> There is no doubt that you have a providential task in this work of understanding and love, a profound work of spiritual reconciliation, of atonement. It is wonderful to realize the full dimension of our priestly calling in the hemisphere. [...] We begin already to heal those to whom we listen. The confusion, hatred, violence, misinformation, blindness of whole populations come from having no one to hear them. Hence they speak with knives, as the Negroes are now doing, for all that has been heard about them is still not them.[42]

Healing begins with listening. But whole populations in the Americas had been systematically silenced for centuries, their identities comfortably constructed and controlled by their oppressors. Unable to make themselves understood or even heard, their inarticulate frustration was beginning to explode in unbounded violence. Martin Luther King, Jr.'s peaceful campaign, although crowned with important civil rights legislation, brought only token integration. In consequence, King's dream of a color-blind society was still only a dream. No wonder that violence was "the language the black America has now elected to speak," as Merton wrote in a 1965 essay, adding that "Black Power was clearly a message that somehow white America *wanted* to hear."[43] It was also the only language white America seemed to understand. Electing to "speak with knives" was an act of desperation, a last plea for being listened to. It is against this background that a Merton's or a Cardenal's "ministry of listening" becomes a healing and providential task.

"What happens to a dream deferred," rhetorically asked Langston Hughes in his 1951 poem entitled "Harlem," warning that in the long run such a dream would inevitably "explode." Had white America listened to his warning, Amiri Baraka might not have had to call for "'poems that kill.'/Assassin poems, Poems that shoot/guns."[44] Malcolm X would not, perhaps, have threatened white America with "the ballot or the bullet" speech. Watts and other race riots might have been avoided. Having observed the development of things in his own country, Merton understood the larger principle at work elsewhere and tried to use the language of non-violence in reparation for his white compatriots' blind reliance on "rituals" of power. Having listened to "all that has not been said" since the beginning of the Conquest, he was prepared to see Indians, as well as Blacks, in terms of America's inner colonies, and developments like the Black Power Movement as part of the struggle of postcolonial countries for self-determination and self-definition. In an essay "Cross Fighters: Notes on a Racial War," for example, he presents the caste conflict in nineteenth-century Yucatán as paradigmatic of the effort of an embattled, radical minority to recover its identity in a modern world it no longer understands.

What Merton says about blacks in "From Non-Violence to Black Power" obviously also applies to his attitude to all the "other" Americans, collectively constituting the repressed, inner American "I" (this category would also include the Asians and other non-white peoples, victims of white imperialist practices):

> [...] I for one remain *for* the Negro, I trust him, I recognize the overwhelming justice of his complaint, I confess I have no right whatever to get in his way, and that as a Christian I owe him support, not in his ranks, but in my own, among the whites who refuse to trust him or hear him, and who want to destroy him.[45]

This passage is an important corrective to Merton's somewhat romantic wish to separate himself "from a civilization that is utterly contemptible and false and heading for its own destruction."[46] However tempting that might be, would it not amount to claiming a sort of "innocent bystander" status at a time when responsibility for and solidarity with the white culture in crisis was called for? Would not Merton's withdrawal from a corrupt society amount to a betrayal of the silent and wise inner child of the collective Adam? When in 1962 Merton's superiors forbade him to speak out on questions of war and peace, he was briefly tempted to disobey, perhaps leave the monastery. However, he immediately realized that his protest against war would be insignificant "unless I can continue to speak from the center of the Church."[47] The same concerned his relationship to the country, as well as its racially divided South: Merton's first duty was to speak on behalf of the other *from the very center of his own society* to make them understand what they were not prepared to hear from the lips of those whom they collectively "othered."

While Merton sincerely hoped that Black people might redeem the United States should it prove able to listen to their prophetic voices, he also expected that the long suppressed "voice of the Andes and of the Amazon,"[48] when finally made audible, would help North America regain its innocence. Only redeemed would the hemisphere have a future. Only then, Merton stressed, would American destiny be fulfilled and "the great cross of our double continent" become the resurrected "Christ of the Americas." "We can and should be prophets of its advent," he urged in a letter to Cuadra.[49] The poetic vocation of Ernesto Cardenal, Pablo Antonio Cuadra, and other "ministers of silence" was to help bring the true American destiny closer to fulfillment.

Merton's idea of poets as monks and ministers of silence comes from Merton's "Message to Poets," an essay he wrote in 1964 for the first inter-American encounter of the New Solidarity Movement of poets launched by Miguel Grinberg, the Argentine writer, translator, and publisher. Grinberg had just founded an organization called Acción Interamericana dedicated to promoting cultural exchange between both parts of the hemisphere and invited Merton to be part of his "literary revolt."[50] To Merton Grinberg's movement was one of the most hopeful signs in the hemisphere, uniting the efforts of poets and other creative Americans to found a spiritual community that would transcend political and economic barriers. The True America was beginning to take shape in this union of creators. By that time Merton had already been attached to Nicaragua's spiritual and literary movement, had been writing essays for publication in diverse Latin American magazines, and translating Latin American poets into English. South of the border he was finding a solid foundation for a more inclusive American culture that could nourish the contemplative life. To one of his Nicaraguan friends he confided: "I feel myself more and more closely united with those who, everywhere, devote themselves [...] to the search for divine values hidden among the poor and the outcast, to the love of that cultural heritage without which man cannot be healthy."[51]

**Fruits of listening**

On September 8, 1960 Merton speculated about the importance of remembering and rethinking the thoughts fundamental to people living in other epochs and other countries. This work of *Memoria* would, obviously, include an effort to retrieve a variety of ancient cultural heritages. But "[i]s it [...] necessary? Is it sane?" he asked, considering the enormous scope of the project. "For me it is an expression of love for man and for God. An expression without which my contemplative life would be senseless."[52] Three years later he was sending Pablo Antonio Cuarda his recent poem-in-progress, "The Early Legend," a fruit of such an attempt. Consisting of "six fragments of work in progress," the poem, as Merton writes, "is still not finished, but it will be a long time before it grows. When it becomes what it is meant to be, it will be quite different, so I think there is no harm in using it now, and it has something vague to say about the basic themes so close to *El Pez y la Serpiente* [sic!]." Destined never to be finished[53] and so forever only a vague anticipation of a larger synthesis, this poem is an invitation to recover what has been lost, to remember the origins and the common heritage of all humanity. Dimly aware of being "the child of a great and peaceful race," the poem's speaker, guided by the beating of drums, enters into a hypnotic trance and merges with cosmic consciousness. In his quest for the ultimate sources of life and wisdom, he "has remembered the whole world at peace [...] the world of villages, of maize, of emeralds, of quiet mothers."[54] This peaceful world, an intuition of primordial reality, is largely—though not exclusively—an anamnesis of pre-historic civilizations of Mesoamerica.

In "The Sacred City," an essay included in the post-humously published collection *Ishi Means Man* and devoted to the Zapotecan Indians' ritual center of Monte Albán and the pre-classical Mayan cities,[55] Merton makes a connection between the essentially peaceful life of pre-historic Indians and the absence of fortified cities. The rise of the city in the post-classical period, Merton claims, was a consequence of the development of commerce and militaristic autocracy. The fortified city gave rise to powerful empires that would conquer neighboring lands and enslave weaker tribes. The sacred city, on the other hand, had been a-historical, therefore basically peaceful ("eventless," since there were no "news" to record in chronicles, no secular events to write about).

In the same essay Merton adds that the "aesthetic and ritual joy" of the neolithic sensuous man provides contrast to technological man's rituals of "work, war, production, domination and brute power."[56] Concluding the essay, he predicts that a modern culture of peace "will have to recover at least something of the values and attitudes that were characteristic of Monte Albán."[57] "The Early Legend" offers poetic-mystical glimpses of such values and attitudes (developed into a more consistent cultural critique in Merton's unfinished long poetic epic *The Geography of Lograire*).

And thus, the image of "quiet mothers," an allusion to the matriarchal stage of societal development, explicitly links the a-historical state of peace with feminine consciousness. The world at peace, then, was the work of Mother Earth or another incarnation of a fertility goddess worshipped in neolithic societies. This goddess seems to reflect the archaic humans' intuition of the divinity of uncreated nature. Merton perceives her as a pre-figuration of *Natura Naturans* or Divine Wisdom. Naturally, as our Sister, she has always delighted in "being with the children of men," and throughout millennia has been crying out "to all who will hear."[58] These have always been predominantly "the little, [...] the ignorant and the helpless."[59] In pre-historic times they were the quiet races of Mesoamerica—the Mayas and the Incas—as well as other neolithic peoples in other parts of the globe (the poem mentions specifically Cretans and Minoans). Most importantly, perhaps, the poem's speaker "remembers" that once the *whole* world was at peace.

Still regressing in time, the poem's persona finally arrives at "the fountains of the spring where the Lord emerges refreshed every morning."[60] This is an image of the origins: the primal innocence of creation, the paradise as it was before the fall, where God lived with and delighted in his creation. And creation was still in the state of primal unity—neither sacred nor secular, above and beyond any divisions, because the Lord, too, says Merton, "is always the familiar person, neither sacred nor secular."[61] This insistence on the Lord's closeness and familiarity betrays a strong influence of Julian of Norwich,[62] who repeatedly called Jesus "Our Mother" and emphasized his *homeliness* (closeness). Thus, the a-historical world "of quiet mothers" emerges as the work of the essentially feminine, *motherly* love of the Lord.

The image of paradisiacal innocence calls to mind America as the New World Garden, a concept established by the first European explorers' descriptions of America's fantastic flora and fauna, and the peaceful disposition of the natives. But this intuition seems to have been around long before the age of geographical discoveries, as confirmed by *Navigatio Sancti Brendani*, a record of the sixth century Celtic monk's journey west, to the "land of promise of the saints." It is not easy to determine whether in writing "The Early Legend" Merton was conscious of these resonances, or given his poetic anamnesis of *the world* at peace, was geography accidental to this vision of earthly paradise. Be it as it may, there is no contradiction between the literal and metaphorical-eschatological reading of the New World Garden: due to its representative racial and ethnic mix, the United States has earned the popular appellation of the nation of nations, an appellation resounding with eschatological implications; Canada has proposed its own model of cultural integration; and the *mestizo* consciousness of Latin America has been hailed as an absolute novelty in human history.[63] It is this mythical,[64] all-embracing America that becomes synonymous with the New World Garden. Would Merton's poem confirm this reading?

Remembering that the New World is often depicted as a cultural crossroads, it should come as no surprise that the poem's speaker—a collective identity by now, a communion of seekers—discovers the Lord in places marked by intercultural encounter:

> We have found places where the Lord of Songs
> visits his beloved. Crossroads. Hilltops. Market towns.
> Ball courts. Harbors. Crossroads. Meeting Places.
> Bridges. Places where the Lord of Songs
> is refreshed. Crossroads.
> It is when the Stranger is met and known
> at the unplanned crossing
> that the Nameless becomes a Name.[65]

All those places are situated outside securely established centers of work or daily, routine existence. They are all the places of risk, uncertainty, instability; sites open to unexpected possibilities, where people of different origin, culture, skin color, religion, etc., mingle and meet. In such chance meetings stereotypical perceptions are challenged, false entrenched believes crumble, the other is *seen*: the anonymous stranger, when met and known *at the unplanned crossing*, acquires a name, becomes a *person*; a relation is established. Now the other is no longer a threat to "my" world, but becomes a revelation of the Nameless One whom the Scriptures present as a wandering God who often appears under the guise of a stranger himself. This might be the value of Merton's American re-vision: if the hemisphere is true to its deepest identity of being a cultural crossroads, strangers will no longer be strange; instead, they will acquire a name, bread will be broken for them, and a free, spiritual "America" will be born. In Merton's powerful poetic vision the poet-narrator immediately recognizes "the silent races" as his brothers and embraces them, and they in turn put their weaponless hands upon his shoulders: "we saw one another in the eye," comments the speaker.[66]

## The land of promise and the reality of the volcano

Not only are the maize-growing Maya, along with other "silent races," among the Lord's beloved, they play their ceremonial ball game on a mountain, which the poem's persona identifies as "our own mountain,"[67] explicitly linking the neolithic ritual centers with the Lord's mountain of the Bible, and their inhabitants with pre-Christian saints. The poem's final fragment discreetly refers back to this idea in the image of "incredible mountains" that "come boiling out of the earth to leave emeralds and gold mixed in the cooling lava."[68] Those are the formidable volcanoes of the Ecuadorian jungle: Volcán Cayambe, Volcán Cotopaxi, Volcán Coliachi, Volcán Sangay. Although Merton perceived the volcano as symbolic of the violence and suffering of historical existence, in the dramatic volcanic eruptions (both literal and metaphorical), he seems to have intuited some "incredible" theophany, as if in consonance with the Herakleitan conviction that all things are fire and transformations of fire.

There are numerous fires in the poem: not all are violent; some are playful, mischievous, seductive. All of them stand for Love, a force gravely misunderstood and actively opposed by humans ("We have not understood their [the fires'] playful modes. We have fought Eros."[69]). These are the fires "of the land promised to my father and mother," says Merton. But this promised land, as he now realizes, is both a new world not yet discovered and "an old world that has never been known."[70] This is an important point which both confirms and elucidates what Merton has been saying in numerous other works; namely, that we are *already* in the promised land, but, at the same time, that this world is present in a humble, "kenotic" way only and so can be seen with the eyes of faith and in the holistic perspective of Wisdom, our Sister. A person of faith knows that God has always been close to humankind-His beloved, seeking her already long before the Incarnation. If we want to retrace His footsteps, we have to reclaim the *whole* of "the old world"—the past of all cultures, and all the wisdoms and religious intuitions scattered throughout human history. Only then will we have sufficient coordinates to arrive at "the new world" of peace and harmonious coexistence, since the old and the new are one. Hence the absolute *obligation* to remember. What is more, however, the task of retrieval would apply predominantly to stories left out of official history books. In "The

Early Legend's" last fragment the poet-shaman has a vision of anonymous strangers ("I do not recognize the names of the men"[71]) who silently, in great simplicity and obscurity of their harsh lives, redeem the apparently unwarranted violence of history—the violence of the volcano—as they "come up out of those fires with diamonds in their hands."[72] Clearly, the revision of history as envisioned by Merton is a re-vision, a new seeing that leads to a new and more comprehensive, more inclusive understanding of the destination of the broadened human journey (the *new* world).

**Conclusion**

Merton's engagement with the Great American Vocation resulted in his heartfelt proclamation of the dawn of a new epoch. This would be the epoch of solidarity and compassion, which, as Merton believed, was gradually becoming conscious of itself in the work of various "artists of life" working toward a new and integrated consciousness. Their struggle to recapture and update the spiritual witness of ancestral cultures was synonymous with turning inward to mine the diamond of their deepest, subconscious heritage; it was a struggle to make the "early legend" return again, a struggle to recover some attitudes of the sacred city. Rediscovering the hidden springs of wisdom among the humblest and the poorest of the earth, those truly *new* Americans were instrumental in bringing about "the great awakening of South America,"[73] which in turn, as Merton believed, would initiate the awakening of the rest of the world. "New consciousness," he wrote in a letter to Miguel Grinberg. "There has to be clean water in the mind for the spirit to drink."[74]

It seems to me that in his visionary anticipation of the new consciousness Merton was subconsciously groping toward a theory of hybrid (*mestizo*) identity and a celebration of heterogeneity, a theme that would need to be carefully researched in its own right. The struggle with his "American" vocation meant for Merton, first of all, a struggle with prejudices and misconceptions, his own as well as his Western culture's; with colonial legacies of exoticism; and post-colonial processes of commodification. In this struggle he was forced to undermine simplistic dichotomies (West, East; New, Old; North, South; etc.) and to recognize that human "roots" are always multiple, that various cultures—various routes—intersect in our lives, and that we are continually being transformed by new encounters.

## Notes

1. Throughout this essay the word "America" will be used in a number of meanings, including—for lack of a better term—the United States of America. Also Merton's "American vocation" will progressively become inclusive of opposites.
2. Merton, Thomas, *The Other Side of the Mountain. The Journals of Thomas Merton.* Vol. 7, ed. Patrick Hart (San Francisco: Harper, 1999), p. 140.
3. Merton, Thomas, *Turning Toward the World. The Journals of Thomas Merton*, Vol. 4, ed. Victor A. Kramer (San Francisco: Harper, 1997), p. 160.
4. Merton, Thomas, *A Search for Solitude. The Journals of Thomas Merton*, Vol. 3, ed. Lawrence S. Cunningham (San Francisco: Harper, 1997), p. 168.
5. Darío, Ruben, "To Roosevelt," transl. Lysander Kemp. *The Borzoi Anthology of Latin American Literature*, ed. E. R. Monegal, vol. 1 (New York: Knopf, 1977), pp. 357-58.
6. This is what Gloria Anzaldúa says about the new *mestiza* (hybrid) consciousness, drawing on José Vasconcelos' theory of the Ibero-American "cosmic" race and its mission. She develops this notion in her book entitled *Borderlands/La Frontera: The New Mestiza* (1987).
7. Clifford, James, *Travel and Translation in the late Twentieth Century* (Cambridge, MA: Harvard University Press, 1997), p. 11. The idea of "roots and routes" as constitutive of cultures also comes from this book.
8. Merton, Thomas, *Entering the Silence. The Journals of Thomas Merton*, vol. 2, ed. Jonathan Montaldo (San Francisco: Harper, 1996), p. 451.
9. Merton, *Entering the Silence*, p. 450.
10. Merton, *Entering the Silence*, p. 451.
11. Merton, *Entering the Silence*, p. 452.
12. Merton, *The Sign of Jonas* (New York: Harcourt, Brace & Co, 1953), p. 330. The fact that this passage is missing from *A Search for Solitude*, the journal from which Merton excerpted *The Sign of Jonas*, indicates that the above passage was a reworking of the experience, an attempt to elucidate its meaning in the light of Merton's "American vocation."
13. Merton, *Entering the Silence*, p. 463.
14. Merton, *Entering the Silence*, p. 464.
15. Merton, *A Search for Solitude*, p. 341.
16. Merton, *A Search for Solitude*, p. 341.
17. Merton, *A Search for Solitude*, p. 341.
18. Merton, *A Search for Solitude*, p. 177.
19. Merton, *A Search for Solitude*, p. 168.
20. Merton, *A Search for Solitude*, p. 169. Merton refers here specifically to the American hemisphere (the New World), but it could be argued that implicitly he is also referring to that larger entity: the western hemisphere. Due to European colonization, the New World is also an extension of the Old World, as much as Merton—born and raised in England and France—embraces the Old and the New. Sometimes the context will determine which meaning is intended; at other times the meaning will remain inclusive.
21. Merton, *A Search for Solitude*, p. 168.

22. Merton, *A Search for Solitude*, p. 169.
23. Merton used this formulation in his letter (August 1, 1963) to Ernesto Cardenal. See Merton, Thomas, *The Courage for Truth. Letters to Writers*, ed. Christine M. Bochen (New York: Farrar, Straus & Girouix, 1993), p. 141.
24. Merton, *A Search for Solitude*, p. 168.
25. Merton, *A Search for Solitude*, p. 299.
26. Merton, Thomas, *Introductions East and West. The Foreign Prefaces of Thomas Merton*, ed. Robert E. Daggy (Greensborough, NC: Unicorn, 1981), p. 35.
27. Merton, Thomas, *Witness to Freedom. Letters in Time of Crisis*, ed. William H. Shannon (New York: Harcourt, Brace & Co, 1994), p. 4. Emphasis added.
28. Merton, *Witness to Freedom*, p. 4.
29. Merton, Thomas, *The Collected Poems of Thomas Merton* (New York: New Directions, 1977), p. 365. Emphasis added.
30. Merton, *A Search for Solitude*, p. 104.
31. Merton, *A Search for Solitude*, p. 114.
32. Merton, *A Search for Solitude*, p. 113.
33. See: Merton, *A Search for Solitude*, p. 231.
34. Cuadra, Pablo Antonio, "Notes para llegar al Indio," inscribed "for Fr. Louis." Archives of the Thomas Merton Center, Bellarmine University, Louisville, KY.
35. Possibly, with all the ambiguities of "oriental" and "occidental" as cultural constructs.
36. Merton, *A Search for Solitude*, p. 200.
37. Merton, *A Search for Solitude*, p. 200.
38. Merton, *A Search for Solitude*, p. 196.
39. Merton, *Collected Poems*, pp. 383-4.
40. Merton, *Courage for Truth*, p. 189.
41. Merton, *Courage for Truth*, p. 146.
42. Merton, *Courage for Truth*, p. 146.
43. Merton, "From Non-Violence to Black Power" in *The Social Essays of Thomas Merton*, ed. William H. Shannon (New York: Crossroads, 1995), p. 211.
44. Baraka, Amiri, "Black Art" in *Anthology of Modern American Poetry*, ed. Cary Nelson (New York, Oxford: Oxford UP, 2000), p. 998.
45. Merton, *The Social Essays*, p. 216.
46. Merton, *A Search for Solitude*, p. 299.
47. Merton, *Turning Toward the World*, p. 244.
48. Merton, letter to Ernesto Cardenal, March 10, 1964, *Courage for Truth*, p. 144.
49. Merton, letter to Pablo Antonio Cuadra, December 4, 1958, *Courage for Truth*, p. 182.
50. Grinberg, Miguel, letter to Merton, May 5, 1963. Archives of the Thomas Merton Center, Bellarmine University, Louisville, KY.
51. Merton, letter to Cuadra, September 16, 1961. *Courage for Truth*, p. 188.
52. Merton, *Turning Toward the World*, pp. 42-3.
53. The poem, with the subtitle "Six Fragments of a Work in Progress," appeared in *Raids on the Unspeakable* (1966) and can also be found in the "Uncollected Poems" section of the *Collected Poems of Thomas Merton*. The poem's unfinished character is most likely attributable

to Merton's realization that a historical synthesis is always premature as long as history is still in progress.

54. Merton, *Collected Poems*, p. 759.

55. Periodization of Mesoamerican history is confusing, because various ancient civilizations were developing at a different pace. For clarity, I will be concerned with the classical and post-classical Maya world only, and will follow the periodization used by Merton and Cardenal. Although the clear-cut distinction between the Old (classical) and the New (post-classical) Kingdom is nowadays contested as simplistic, according to mid 20th century sources the transition from one to the other was marked by the arrival of the militaristic Toltec people (ca. 900 CE) who transformed the peaceful Maya world into an atheistic culture identified with secular wealth, and warrior, rather than theocratic, aristocracy.

56. Merton, *Ishi Means Man* (Greensboro UC, Unicorn, 1976), p. 65.

57. Merton, *Ishi*, p. 71.

58. Merton, "Hagia Sophia," in *Collected Poems*, p. 368.

59. Merton, *Collected Poems*, p. 364.

60. Merton, *Collected Poems*, p. 762.

61. Merton, *Collected Poems*, p. 763. On September 11, 1965 Merton writes: "My space is the world created and redeemed by God, and God is in this true world, not 'only' and restrictively a prisoner in the monastery. [...] my task is to get rid of the last vestiges of a pharisaical division between the sacred and the secular, and to see that the *whole* world is reconciled to God in Christ, not just the monastery, nor only the convents, the churches, and the good Catholic schools." *Dancing in the Water of Life. The Journals of Thomas Merton*, vol. 5, ed. Robert E. Daggy (San Francisco: Harper, 1997), pp. 293-94.

62. In 1961 Merton writes about the "real discovery" of Lady Julian. *Turning Toward the World*, p. 189.

63. Pietri, Arturo Uslar writes: "What happened in Spanish America . . . resembles nothing that occurred on other continents in the encounters between Europeans and natives. It did not happen in North America, or Africa or Asia in the spheres of English or French control." See Pietri, "The Other America," in *Oxford Book of Latin American Essays*, ed. Illa Stavans (New York: Oxford University Press, 1979), p. 211. See also Anzaldúa's *Borderlands*.

64. Mythical in the sense of what it stands for, rather than what is actually is.

65. Merton, *Collected* Poems, p. 763.

66. Merton, *Collected Poems*, p. 763.

67. Merton, *Collected Poems*, p. 763.

68. Merton, *Collected Poems*, p. 767.

69. Merton, *Collected Poems*, p. 767.

70. Merton, *Collected Poems*, p. 767.

71. Merton, *Collected Poems*, p. 767.

72. Merton, *Collected Poems*, p. 767.

73. Merton, letter to Ernesto Cardenal, March 10, 1964, *Courage for Truth*, p. 144.

74. Merton, letter to Miguel Grinberg, October 28, 1966, *Courage for Truth*, p. 204.

# THOMAS MERTON'S CONTEMPLATION
Rarefied Emblem of Being Human and Living in Mystery

Glenn Crider

### Robust contemplation

With references to Zen Buddhism, Augustine of Hippo (354-430 C.E.) and Ludwig Wittgenstein (1889-1951), this examination demonstrates the importance of Thomas Merton's understanding of contemplation which embodies the rare combination of ancient, medieval, modern and post-modern sensibilities. I emphasize *sensibilities* in order to avoid categorizing Merton strictly as this or that, but also to emphasize his intense desire to integrate life into a single whole and the significance of this fact. Like his monastic life and work, Merton's best contemplative writing reveals his amazing ability to draw from a variety of Christian and non-Christian sources. Further, as he grew and developed within his monastic community, Merton became more and more open to the world itself—as a place of mystery and wonder. That openness stems from his desire and successful ability to implement his monastic identity through the use of countless Christian and non-Christian sources. This characteristic feature underscores Merton's contemplative life as an example of one who "seeks after God" while such seeking allowed the mature Merton to elude a myriad of religious and spiritual pigeonholes and illusions. Consequently, Thomas Merton remains a great awakener for those who choose to attune themselves to his life and work.

Merton's final writings about contemplation portray his struggle to integrate such writing with the contemplative life, that is, with life itself. William H. Shannon notes that *The Inner Experience: Notes on*

*Contemplation*[1] began as a revision of *What Is Contemplation?*[2] which was published in 1948—seven years after Merton had entered the Abbey of Gethsemani. In 1959, however, Merton began to rewrite *What Is Contemplation?* On July 12, 1959, he wrote in his journal that his revisions of *What Is Contemplation?* were three times as long and a "completely different book."[3] Merton indicates why he made such drastic changes to that text: "A lot of water has gone under the bridge since 1948. How poor were all my oversimplified ideas—and how mistaken I was to make contemplation only *part* of [one's] life. For a contemplative [one's] whole life is contemplation."[4] Following *What Is Contemplation?*'s metamorphosis into *The Inner Experience*, Merton wrote four separate drafts of *The Inner Experience* in 1959. The "final" revisions did not occur, however, until 1968 (the year of Merton's death).

As Shannon indicates, the fourth draft of *The Inner Experience* was eventually published. In 1968, Merton made a final series of revisions and additions to that draft. A curious event occurred a year earlier, however, when Merton authorized the Merton Legacy Trust to publish his manuscripts that had not been published.[5] He explicitly excluded two manuscripts from this agreement. One was "The Inner Experience." The only way material from this manuscript could be published was if "qualified scholars" wanted to quote from it.[6]

Allowing scholars to quote from *The Inner Experience* shows that Merton limited its availability to a select few, and he prohibited its publication in any comprehensive format—especially as a book. At least this was the case until 1968 when Daniel Walsh—Merton's philosophy teacher at Columbia—wrote a letter to Gethsemani's abbot, suggesting that Merton had a change of heart about publishing *The Inner Experience*. Merton had gone to Bellarmine College on May 14, 1968 to give Walsh a gift for his one-year anniversary to the priesthood. The gift was a copy of *The Inner Experience*. Merton told Walsh: "[This] is something I wrote a long time ago, but [I wonder] what the response to it would be if it were published. I had previously decided against it [in the Merton Legacy Trust]. But recently I reread it and made some corrections and additions which you will note in this copy."[7] Shannon believes that Merton's remark about something he wrote "a long time ago" refers to those drafts of *The Inner Experience*, written during the summer of 1959.[8] Despite the nine years it took for Merton to decide that *The Inner Experience* might be worthy of publication, Walsh's letter to Father Flavian Burns convinced Father Flavian that the book in fact should be published.

The Inner Experience is one of Merton's last "standard" writings on contemplation. In addition to *What Is Contemplation?* (1948), *Seeds of Contemplation* (1949) and *New Seeds of Contemplation* (1961) stand as standard works as well. *The Climate of Monastic Prayer*, better known as *Contemplative Prayer*, was published posthumously in 1969. It too is a standard writing. *The Inner Experience*, however, likely represents Merton's most robust account of contemplation. Shannon suggests that, except for the few corrections and additions of 1968, the work belongs to the year 1959.[9] Therefore,

> it may be seen as a "bridge" between the early and later Merton. In this work he makes clear that contemplation is not a compartment of life, but rather the way to integrate one's life into a single whole.... There are clear indications of his "return to the world" with a sense of compassion for people that clearly marks a departure from the excessive "world-denying position" of some of the earlier writings.[10]

Merton's 1968 revisions cannot be underestimated in terms of qualifying a nine-year-old manuscript for publication. What makes *The Inner Experience* unique is that, in addition to being a "bridge" between the early and later Merton, it is also the final contemplative writing bearing Merton's approval as of 1968. The value of this work is that it reflects Merton's mature position on contemplation, one that does not limit itself to *writing* about contemplation.

*The Inner Experience* as an unfinished work, ironically, is Merton's ideal contemplative writing. It demonstrates the problem of attempting to use language to express the inexpressible. Consequently, Merton paradoxically directs readers away from his writings and toward that which "shows" Merton's contemplative character. This précis about how *The Inner Experience* developed emphasizes a prolific writer's struggle and toil over writing about contemplation. Intertwined with this emphasis is the point that Merton uses outlets other than writing to demonstrate what contemplation is, which he describes as the "highest expression" of one's intellectual and spiritual life.[11]

## Necessary distinctions

In light of the introductory foundation of this article, which provides a basis for understanding Merton's approach to writing about contemplation, two key distinctions must be made: Merton's standard contemplative *writings* reveal a Christian epistemology that is largely ancient and medieval. Merton *the contemplative*, on the other hand, reveals a postmodern "seeker," who embraces the limits of language, for example, through solitude, art and social action. I rely on Augustine and Wittgenstein in order to shed atypical light on the complexity and compelling character of Merton's contemplation. One point of this approach is to emphasize Merton's realization of the need to use multiple ways for understanding contemplation. Another point is to show how Merton's contemplative writings compare to strands within the Western development of theological and philosophical thought that necessarily involves "self-knowledge" and "knowledge of God." The overall "picture" of Merton's inquiries into contemplation embodies what he understood as the very essence of being human. Understanding this essence is necessary for knowing what Merton means by "contemplation."

Following his belief that contemplation integrates life into a single whole, Merton provides a starting point for understanding the essence of being human: "The meaning of my life is not to be looked for merely in the sum total of my own achievements. It is seen only in the complete integration of my achievements and failures with the achievements and failures of my own generation, and society, and time. It is seen, above all, in my integration in the mystery of Christ."[12] Here, Merton offers a clue for understanding what he means by integrating life into a single whole. It involves recognizing oneself as inherently integrated within one's own culture and with other individuals. This interpretation of "self" is a radical challenge both to Western individualism and to common misconceptions about the contemplative life as a solitary state of "interiority."

*The Inner Experience* uses Zen language to critique Western language about the "self." Any Zen discussion of the "self," Merton says, begins beyond the Western division between *"self and not-self."*[13] Contrary to Merton's criticism of the Western division of "self and not-self," or of subject and object, it is precisely a critique of this so-called "division" that is a focus of much classical German philosophy (1781-1844).[14]

Clearly, in light of Merton's relationship to poetry, it is significant that much of the romantic theory of art and poetry originated from the early romantics' interpretation and application of Fichte's *Science of Knowledge*. Merton's fascination with William Blake is a good reminder of his early and continuing conviction(s) about mystical insights.

The "real self" in Zen seeks nothing beyond its immediate experience. Merton recalls the experience of a Chinese official under the Sung dynasty, who realized his "real self" in such an immediate way: "Chao-pien was sitting there at peace when he heard a clap of thunder, and the 'mind doors burst open,' in the depths of his silent being, to reveal his 'original self,' or '*suchness.*' The whole incident is summarized, according to Chinese custom, in a four-line poem, and it has rightly become immortal"[15]:

> *Devoid of thought, I sat quietly by the desk in my official room,*
> *With my fountain-mind undisturbed, as serene as water;*
> *A sudden crash of thunder, the mind doors burst open,*
> *And lo, there sits the old man in all his homeliness.*[16]

Merton is attracted to Zen because it makes no claims to be "supernatural or mystical."[17] Zen is therefore anti-metaphysical.

The mature Merton's interest in Zen is significant because Zen contrasts so much with the ancient and medieval metaphysical traditions within Merton's standard contemplative writings. For example, drawing explicitly from Pseudo-Dionysius and St. John of the Cross, Merton epitomizes Augustine's legacy of describing the relationship between God and humanity as rooted in "being":

> Contemplation is the work of love, and the contemplative proves his love by leaving all things, even the most spiritual things, for God in nothingness, detachment, and "night." But the deciding factor in contemplation is the free and unpredictable action of God. He alone can grant the gift of mystical grace and make Himself known by the secret, ineffable contact that reveals His presence in the depths of the soul. What counts is not the soul's love for God, but God's love for the soul.[18]

This passage exemplifies Merton's frequent "metaphysical" descriptions of the contemplative life. His emphasis on God's love for the soul is Augustinian, but it also reflects the apophatic theology of early and medieval mystics.

To articulate his contemplative spirituality, Merton draws heavily from Augustine's Platonic-Christian portrayal of the relationship between God and humanity. Merton's reliance upon Augustine is no surprise, of course. In light of Augustine's influence upon Western Christianity, it is to be expected that Merton depend upon Augustine.

Augustine's influence starts with Merton's language itself. Merton's language throughout his standard contemplative works is therefore decidedly Augustinian. In such texts there is much explicit talk about "Christian love," "Love," "Trinity," "faith," "faith in Christ," "knowledge of God," "God," "God's love," "purity of heart," "the Spirit," "soul," etc. Augustine's *De Trinitate* bears this kind of language. So comparing Merton and Augustine by way of a simple word search shows striking similarities. One might say that Merton's language is "Christian," which is to say that it is more or less Augustinian, for Augustine set the literal terms for Western theology. And it is Augustine who penned the first Christian autobiography—*The Confessions*. Some argue that *The Confessions* is not an "autobiography" per se, but a theological argument. Regardless, the text set the stage for writing about oneself within a Christian framework. In fact, Merton's *The Seven Storey Mountain* holds the unofficial title of "the twentieth-century version of Augustine's *Confessions*."[19] (We know Merton owned a copy of *The Confessions* which was heavily annotated.) Merton's contemplative writings share his autobiographical spirit in *The Seven Storey Mountain* in the sense that Merton himself grapples with contemplation by way of writing.

In addition to language and autobiographical form, the roots of Merton's contemplative philosophy are also Augustinian. For example, Merton's states, "Because God's love is in me, it can come to you from a different and special direction that would be closed if He did not live in me, and because His love is in you, it can come to me from a quarter from which it would not otherwise come. And because it is in both of us, God has greater glory."[20] This passage echoes Book VIII of Augustine's *De Trinitate*, where the soul must direct itself toward loving in the "right" way, or by seeking to know God by loving one's neighbor appropriately. Augustine's identification of goodness with God ontically connects human knowing, willing, and loving to God. And this connection is made possible through Trinitarian love. Both Merton and Augustine use language of *intentionality* in the sense that the individual must seek for him or herself the love of God. Such seeking is paradoxical, however, because one cannot "achieve" or "attain" the love of God. Rather, it becomes possible only through grace. Nonetheless, their *intentional* language suggests a dual process involving passivity and activity in the "search for God."

Emphasizing both passivity and activity, Merton states, "Faith is not just conformity, it is *life* . . . . Until [one] yields [oneself] to God in the consent of total belief, [one] must inevitably remain a stranger to [oneself] . . . because [one] is excluded from the most meaningful depths of [one's] own being . . . ."[21] The driving force behind both Merton and Augustine is "faith." Faith is how humans "connect" with God, and faith is made possible through God's grace. Their implied philosophical position asserts an "ontic" connection between humanity and God. That is, both writers assume some sort of relationship with God that is "real" through a "relational" awareness. The justification of such a position rests on belief in the human soul and its relational connection to God.

Beginning with study of Augustine and extending to, for example, the Desert Fathers, Pseudo-Dionysius, St. Bernard of Clairvaux, Meister Eckhart, St. John of the Cross, and St. Teresa of Avila, Merton envisions the modern contemplative as one who can profit from being aware of the importance of pre-modern contemplatives. These figures represent aspects of the diverse theological tradition of the "inner way" that holds so much influence on the development of Western Christian thought. Key to this tradition for the contemplative is the correlation of the mind's knowledge of itself and the knowledge of God. C. Marius Victorinus and Clement of Alexandria introduced this correlation to speculative Christian theology. And Augustine's theoretical explorations of self-knowledge and the knowledge of God achieved near hegemony within Western Christianity.

Merton's use of pre-modern monasticism and mysticism builds on Augustine's explorations of self-knowledge in a way that anticipates Merton's interest in Zen. In *The Inner Experience*, Merton uses several chapters to discuss different kinds of contemplation, problems and dangers of contemplation, and warnings about contemplation and its paradoxical character. In the first chapter, "A Preliminary Warning," he states that if the reader seeks contemplation and happiness and is "intent on 'becoming a contemplative' you will probably waste your time and do yourself considerable harm by reading this book."[22] Merton also stresses that *The Inner Experience* is not an "inspirational" book and that Eastern traditions have the advantage of disposing one more naturally for contemplation.[23] Merton is aware that Western Christianity's development of the "inner way" metamorphoses repeatedly, and such radical changes result in the ongoing need to rethink and reconfigure what it means to be a contemplative.

**Dynamism and openness**
To be a contemplative, or to be fully human, Merton shows through his life and work that being dynamic and open creates opportunities that would be unavailable otherwise. As a Cistercian, Merton certainly embraced his monastic identity. Much can be said about his dutiful commitment and obedience to the Church and his monastic brothers within the Abbey of Gethsemani. Yet his commitment and obedience did not prevent him from "seeking God" outside of, say, the cloistered walls of Gethsemani, the Catholic Church, or even Christianity.

The utter contrast between the Augustinian and the Zen "self," which Merton wrestles with in *The Inner Experience*, demonstrates his unwillingness simply to accept a traditional Christian view of contemplation. That is, Merton certainly "accepts" the significance of Augustine's "ontological" self, but his acceptance allows him to explore what it means to be a "self" in relation to competing Christian sources as well as non-Christian sources. The value of Merton in this regard is that he shares his life with anyone who wishes to develop his or her own sense of self in the rigorous way that is characteristic of Merton.

Clearing Merton from any post-modern affiliations, Robert Inchausti suggests that Merton's understanding of the self is ultimately ontological.[24] If Merton holds to such a position, then he stands, Inchausti argues, as a twentieth-century Christian apostle who is "absolutely paradoxically, teleologically placed."[25] The emphasis here is upon Merton's role as a modern *Christian* contemplative who rejects post-modern and post-structuralist theories of the "self." According to Inchausti, the key distinction between Merton and post-modern theorists such as Jacques Lacan or Jacques Derrida regards "alienation."[26] In *Zen and the Birds of Appetite*, Merton argues that

> another, metaphysical, consciousness is still available to [us]. It starts not from the thinking and self-aware subject but from Being, ontologically seen to be beyond and prior to the subject-object division. Underlying the subjective experience of the individual self, there is an immediate awareness of Being. This is totally different from an experience of self-consciousness . . . . It has in it none of the split and alienation that occurs when the subject becomes aware of itself as a quasi-object.[27]

The "split and alienation" of the subject refers to certain post-modern interpretations of the self, which Merton obviously rejects. The "metaphysical consciousness" that Merton alludes to is one that builds upon the pre-modern sense of self yet without committing to a Kantian awareness of self. So, Merton affirms yet again Augustine's basic premise that "Being" makes awareness of the self possible, and such Being is essentially God.

Despite Merton's assertions of a Westernized ontological self, however, he frequently considers other forms of the self in *The Inner Experience*:

> The intellectual and Platonizing speculations of St. Augustine put us in a very different experiential climate from what we have . . . discussed in Zen, and it is therefore not easy to say where to place the "inmost self" of which Augustine speaks. There is always a possibility that what an Eastern mystic describes as Self is what the Western mystic will describe as God, because we shall see presently that the mystical union between the soul and God renders them in some sense "undivided" (though metaphysically distinct) in spiritual experience. And the fact that the Eastern mystic, not conditioned by centuries of theological debate, may not be inclined to reflect on the fine points of metaphysical distinction

does not necessarily mean that he has not experienced the presence of God when he speaks of knowing the Inmost Self.[28]

Here, Merton provides a glimpse of his affinity for Zen as he suggests that "knowing God" is possible in a variety of ways.

As much as Merton favors and draws from pre-modern Christian theology, his discussions of Zen stand as a criticism of certain problems within contemporary Christian approaches to the contemplative life. A key problem that Merton addresses is, as already mentioned, the subject-object duality in Western conceptions of the self. He sees Zen as a way out of this duality because such a thing simply does not exist in Zen. This duality does not exist because Zen "resolutely refuses to answer clearly, abstractly, or dogmatically any religious or philosophical question whatever."[29] To spell out this difference between Zen and Christian contemplation, Merton provides a question-and-answer illustration in which the Zen masters deliberately frustrate their disciples who keep inserting abstract doctrines "in between the mind and the 'this' which was right before their nose"[30]:

> Someone asked Yakusan, who was sitting in meditation, "What are you doing here?"
> He replied, "I am not doing anything."
> "If so, you are sitting in idleness."
> "Sitting in idleness is doing something."
> "You say you are not doing anything, but what is this 'anything' that you are not doing?"
> "Even the ancient sages know not," replied Yakusan.[31]

Here Merton underscores a vital point about this illustration: "And when disciples asked the Zen masters, 'What is the meaning of Zen?' hoping for a doctrinal exposition, they would get in reply, 'How do I know?' or 'Ask the post over there.' Or 'Zen is that cypress tree in the courtyard!'"[32] In contrast to Merton's ontological understanding of "self," his understanding of faith "does not lead to the recovery of any ontology but to the transformation of life and of human relations in the light of a God who is outside any predication, who is not a being but wholly other."[33] Through this Zen-like illustration, Merton reminds

Christians that being in relationship with God transcends religious traditions or philosophical categories. "Knowing God" requires recognizing the significance of *immediate* experience in contrast to the limitations of metaphysical beliefs.

Commenting on his enthusiasm for Zen, Merton remarks, "Zen is saying, as Wittgenstein said, 'Don't think: Look!'"[34] For Wittgenstein, the difference between "thinking" and "looking" is clear. "Thinking" is deceptive. "Looking" is reliable. Wittgenstein favors the physical act of looking over "thinking," which is clearly why Merton associates his reference to Wittgenstein with Zen. It is ironic that Merton references Wittgenstein in this way, however. Merton states, "The whole aim of Zen is not to make foolproof statements about experience, but to come to direct grips with reality without the mediation of logical verbalizing."[35] A basic point of Wittgenstein's is that one cannot access the "human mind" non-linguistically, or without language. For Wittgenstein, "gripping reality" without the mediation of language is a *philosophical* endeavor, which takes for granted its own use of language. Thus, the Zen attempt to grasp reality without language is, in fact, a *metaphysical* exercise.

The contemporary commentator, Fergus Kerr, depicts Wittgenstein's emphasis on "our life," on "action," and on the human being in a way that clearly complements Merton's awareness of the dangers of a metaphysically based contemplative life that does not recognize the importance of immediate experience and social engagement:

> The metaphysical tradition just *is* the disavowal of the mundane world of conversation and collaboration in which human life consists. In countless, often almost invisible, ways, the metaphysically generated fantasy of the human estranges us from ourselves. The aim of Wittgenstein's "spiritual exercises" is to liberate us from that disseminated antipathy to bodiliness which is the last remnant of heretical theology in what we are naturally inclined, in moments of reflection, to say about ourselves and our relationships with one another.[36]

The mature Merton holds such criticism of metaphysics in tension along with his Augustinian view of "being."

Wittgenstein argues that the function of language contains the possibility of creating monstrous illusions such as "objective metaphysical realities" or "subjective states of consciousness." Both are mistaken products of what is actually "given," which is the logic of language. So, the rules that govern the collective and individual human activity of "making sense" are strictly linguistic, to which Wittgenstein alludes:

> Thought does not strike us as mysterious while we are thinking, but only when we say, as it were retrospectively: "How was that possible?" How was it possible for thought to deal with the very object *itself*? We feel as if by means of it we had caught reality in our net.[37]

Because we cannot "catch reality in our net," Wittgenstein radicalizes Kant's prescription that "we are neither suspended from heaven nor anchored on earth," by suggesting that Kant's dilemma has less to do with our position in the world and more to do with the more bewitching dilemma of *speaking meaningfully* about our position in the world.

Wittgenstein's *Tractatus Logico-Philosophicus* starkly divides what can and cannot be said. For example, "That which expresses *itself* in language, *we* cannot express by language . . . . What *can* be shown *cannot* be said."[38] Here Wittgenstein alludes to the logic of language, which is transcendental and therefore cannot be said. This logic nonetheless "shows itself" through its manifestation within language. Contrasting the *Tractatus* with his (much later) *Philosophical Investigations*, Wittgenstein shifts from dividing between "what can and cannot be said" to stating "it is wrong to say," respectively. For example, Wittgenstein says in *Philosophical Investigations*, "It is correct to say 'I know what you are thinking,' and wrong to say 'I know what I am thinking.'"[39] Moreover, "When philosophers use words—'knowledge,' 'being,' 'object,' 'I,' 'proposition,' 'name'—and try to grasp the *essence* of the thing, one must always ask oneself: is the word ever actually used in this way in the language which is its original home?—What *we* do is to bring words back from their metaphysical to their everyday use."[40] To nuance the *Tractatus*, *Philosophical Investigations* amplifies the danger of speaking in certain ways. The point is not so much that one literally cannot say this or that, but being aware of the use of language and its limitations is necessary. Consequently, one may begin to speak in different, more meaningful ways.

Merton is likewise aware of the dangers of speaking about the "essence" of contemplation. *The Inner Experience* is witness to Merton's awareness of Wittgenstein's distinctions between language and philosophy, and the known and unknown. In fact, the Cartesian roots of the title itself—"The Inner Experience"—encounter criticism as Merton works through the history of contemplation both in Western and Eastern forms. As much as Merton discusses the significance of "self" and "consciousness," he says that one of the most important needs for "Christian consciousness" is one's "liberation from his inordinate self-consciousness, his monumental self-awareness, his obsession with self-affirmation, so that he may enjoy the freedom from concern that goes with being simply what he is and accepting things as they are in order to work with them as he can."[41] It takes time to absorb what Merton means by this, but it is obvious that he considers Zen and figures such as Wittgenstein who have wrestled with language limitations to be important for Christians to develop their sense of self.

**Christian and non-Christian invitations to mystery**
The point of comparing and contrasting Augustine to Wittgenstein and Christianity to Zen is to demonstrate that Merton takes seriously both Christian and non-Christian sources for his own contemplative engagement. It is not about determining, for example, whether Augustine or Wittgenstein is "right" or "wrong," or if Zen is incompatible with Christianity. The tendency, of course, is to make such judgments. But Merton does not. He shows that it is possible to *live* a deeply committed life without compromising one's ability to ask difficult questions that, in many cases, have no *real* answers. Like Augustine and Wittgenstein, Merton never states that he "found the solution" to life or that he "knows the answer" to the mystery of who we are.

Instead Merton invites us to live in mystery. The challenge to living this way is to be willing to develop and change in response to faith. Merton certainly lived this way throughout his monastic career. When he entered Gethsemani in 1941, as a pious Catholic convert and new member of the austere Trappists, it is unlikely that he was aware of the inchoate nature of his identity. Yet Merton progressed day-by-day, evolving and changing in response to a variety of individual and collective needs and desires. As a result, he became someone quite different from the person of certainty in his early monastic career.

Merton's radical metamorphosis as monk and writer is his contribution to those who want to live the kind of life that he says is available to all. Merton provides a "picture" of what the contemplative life looks like. This "picture" contains twenty-seven years of transformation that is complex, multifaceted, and paradoxical. Above all Merton's picture of contemplation (of life lived fully awake) is honest. Merton does not hide his frustrations and disappointments nor does he embellish his happiness and joy.

In his Introduction to *The Inner Experience*, Shannon suggests that Merton never intended to write a comprehensive treatment of contemplation that would be complete and definitive. Merton did not attempt to write such a text because he believed it to be impossible to do so. Shannon's subtle yet descriptive observation reveals a critical reason why Merton remains an invaluable source for understanding contemplation: Merton's life as a whole demonstrates what contemplation *is* and what it is not. Contemplation definitely is not captured in Merton's writings. Instead his writings simply allude to contemplation. One must look at how Merton's contemplative writings intertwine with his monastic life of prayer, social engagement, meditation, correspondence, teaching, writing poetry, religious devotion, photography, and art. In other words, Merton's contemplative writings fall short when read in isolation, or apart from his multifaceted contemplative life. And that is a fundamental point that *The Inner Experience* makes in both explicit and implicit ways. To resist the Western tendency merely to read about contemplation, one must attentively follow Merton's directive that contemplation integrates human life into a single whole.

Merton's juxtaposition of Zen Buddhism and Christianity, of figures such as Augustine and Wittgenstein, reflects his desire to integrate life into a single whole, which means living in a way that moves beyond the individual and toward the collective. One's own "achievements and failures" therefore become the "achievements and failures" of one's generation, and society, and time. Plato's *Symposium* and the *Phaedrus* introduces *eros* as a force eternally striving to grasp the "whole," but always failing to reach this goal. The paradox of Merton's twenty-seven-year "picture" of contemplation is that it never captures the full "essence" of contemplation because, for the contemplative, life itself cannot be grasped in any essential way, yet, paradoxically, in contemplation life is.

**Notes**

1. Merton, Thomas, *The Inner Experience: Notes on Contemplation*, ed. William H. Shannon (San Francisco: HarperCollins, 2003).
2. The 1948 version of *What Is Contemplation?* is a pamphlet written by Merton in response to a student at St. Mary's College, Notre Dame, who had asked Merton, "What is Contemplation?" The pamphlet became a "book" in 1950 and was published in the United States by Templegate, and in Europe by Burns and Oates of London.
3. Merton, Thomas, *A Search for Solitude: The Journals of Thomas Merton, Volume Three 1952-1960*, ed. Lawrence S. Cunningham (San Francisco: HarperSanFrancisco, 1996), p. 303.
4. Merton, *A Search for Solitude*, p. 303.
5. See Merton, *The Inner Experience*, pp. ix ff.
6. See Merton, *The Inner Experience*, p. x.
7. Quoted in Merton, *The Inner Experience*, p. xi.
8. Merton, *The Inner Experience*, p. xi.
9. Merton, *The Inner Experience*, p. xiv.
10. Merton, *The Inner Experience*, p. xiv.
11. See Merton, Thomas, *New Seeds of Contemplation* (New York: New Directions, 1961), p. 1.
12. Inchausti, Robert, *Thomas Merton's American Prophecy* (Albany, NY: State University of New York Press, 1998), p. 141.
13. Merton, *The Inner Experience*, p. 9.
14. The sixty-three-year period "between Kant and Hegel" offers critical insight regarding many problems of subjectivity. The work of German philosopher, Johann Gottlieb Fichte (1762-1814), who attempted to correct problems in the Kantian system, namely, the gap between the moral law and subjectivity as well as the division of theoretical and practical reason, focuses explicitly on the Kantian division of subject and object. Thinking itself is "practical," for Fichte, which implies that the activity of the "I" is not dependent upon a theoretical apprehension of truth or morality. Instead, the "I" determines for itself what it means to live in freedom. In his search for a first Principle of Consciousness, Fichte discovers that consciousness depends upon an "act" (*Thathandlung*), which allegedly undermines the Kantian system that merely asserts a "fact" (*Thatsache*) of consciousness. Fichte's First Principle of Consciousness argues that "subject" and "object" are inherently unified. See Fichte's *The Science of Knowledge*, edited by Peter Heath and John Lachs (Cambridge: Cambridge University Press, 1982).
15. Merton, *The Inner Experience*, p. 9.
16. Merton, *The Inner Experience*, p. 9.
17. Merton, *The Inner Experience*, p. 8.
18. Merton, *The Inner Experience*, p. 73.

19. This "title" appears in many editions of *The Seven Storey Mountain*, typically on the back cover.
20. Merton, *New Seeds of Contemplation*, p. 67.
21. Merton, *New Seeds of Contemplation*, p. 137.
22. Merton, *The Inner Experience*, pp. 2-3.
23. Merton, *The Inner Experience*, p. 3.
24. Inchausti, pp. 131-40.
25. Inchausti, p. 140.
26. Inchausti, pp. 132 ff.
27. Merton, Thomas, *Zen and the Birds of Appetite* (New York: New Directions, 1968), pp. 23-24.
28. Merton, *The Inner Experience*, p. 13.
29. Merton, *The Inner Experience*, p. 20.
30. Merton, *The Inner Experience*, p. 20.
31. Merton, *The Inner Experience*, p. 21.
32. Merton, *The Inner Experience*, p. 21.
33. Inchausti, p. 116.
34. Merton, *Zen and the Birds of Appetite*, p. 49.
35. Merton, *Zen and the Birds of Appetite*, p. 37.
36. Kerr, Fergus, *Theology After Wittgenstein*, 2nd edition (London: SPCK, 1997), pp. 140-41.
37. Wittgenstein, Ludwig, *Philosophical Investigations* (Malden, MA: Blackwell, 2001), § 428.
38. Wittgenstein, Ludwig, *Tractatus Logico-Philosophicus* (New York: Dover Publications, 1999), 4.121, 4.1212.
39. Wittgenstein, *Philosophical Investigations*, p. 189.
40. Wittgenstein, *Philosophical Investigations*, § 116.
41. Merton, *Zen and the Birds of Appetite*, p. 31.

# EXCERPTS FROM THE INTERNATIONAL THOMAS MERTON SOCIETY GENERAL MEETING (2005) AND THE AMERICAN BENEDICTINE ACADEMY CONVENTION (2008)

[From] Thomas Merton, Monk and Prophet of Peace: The Opening Address at the 2005 International Thomas Merton Society General Meeting[1]

John Eudes Bamberger

...[F]rom my first contact with Merton's writings, I viewed him as a prophetic voice for our times. In fact, I believe that Merton himself, already before he entered the monastery, was convinced he had a special gift to speak in God's name to his age. That is what accounts for his beginning to write an autobiography already at the age of twenty-four, shortly after his conversion. This conviction led him to break with a tradition of centuries and to overcome the initial resistance of his superiors, by publishing a journal, *The Sign of Jonas*, about his day-to-day experiences and reflections as a Trappist monk not long after publication of his life story.

He continues to speak to us today in circumstances that, in many respects, are marked by the issues he identified half a century ago as crucial for the future of our world. His life and writings that have brought us together here in the cause of Christian faith and world peace are a living indication of his role as one who speaks in the name of the God of peace and justice. His concern for these issues was a fruit of the faith that grew out of his monastic life and contemplative prayer. Rightly to understand his approach to the issues of peace and non-violence, it is essential to advert to the fact that his chief, daily efforts were expended in what the monastic tradition calls, "the work of the heart," that is, the prolonged struggle with the passions and contemplative assimilation of the truths of faith. Through this interior labor he became, as Gordan Zahn notes, a man "ahead of his time" because he was "in tune with his time."

Merton viewed his times in the light of history. This perspective permitted him to observe with keen penetration that "somewhere in the last fifty years we have crossed a mysterious limit set by Providence and have entered a new era...There has been a violent disruption of society and a radical overthrow of that modern world which goes back to Charlemagne." Based on his contemplative experience he viewed the issues of war and violence in the broadest of contexts, as a crisis of the spirit as he stated in 1962:

> The present world crisis is not merely a political and economic conflict. It goes deeper than ideologies. It is a crisis of [humanity's] spirit. It is a great religious and moral upheaval of the human race, and we do not really know half the causes of this upheaval. We cannot pretend to have a full understanding of what is going on in ourselves and in our society...The moral evil in the world is due to [humanity's] alienation from the deepest truth, from the springs of spiritual life within [one]self.

Anyone who reads some of the many books and articles written about Merton the man and his thought, will soon realize that he was uncommonly sensitive to the social forces at work in his world and so was able to interpret its condition and spiritual needs with an exactitude of insight. It will also be apparent that he was a many-sided personality, richly complex, not always obviously consistent in his opinions.

**Note**
1. The other keynote speaker was John Dear, S.J. See *The Merton Annual: Studies in Culture, Spirituality, and Social Concerns*, Vol. 19 (Louisville, NY: Fons Vitae, 2007), pp. 24-38

# [From the conclusion of] "Sharing the Experience of the Divine Light": Thomas Merton's Path to Inter-religious Understanding; Encounters and Dialogues with Muslims

**Sidney H. Griffith**

The networks within which we have reviewed Thomas Merton's encounters and dialogues with Muslims may well stand as a paradigm for many of his inter-religious engagements. They all began on the personal level and evolved in some instances into a level of familiarity that even yielded important publications. One thinks in this connection, for example, of books such as Merton's *Mystics and Zen Masters*[1] or *The Way of Chuang-Tzu*.[2] They reveal the depth of Merton's inter-religious empathy and his capacity to experience the "other" from within. In this way he was able to bring his largely Christian readers into the world of Zen Buddhists, Taoists, and Muslims in ways that not only would help them to gain an authentic sense of the "other" but even to see how knowledge of the "other" might aid a deeper development of their own Christian faith. This is readily evident in Merton's involvement with Muslims, albeit that he never wrote a book called *Mystics and Sufi Masters*.

As we have seen, Merton came into what we might call his "Islamic consciousness" through his correspondence with Louis Massignon, which led him very soon into his correspondence with Abdul Aziz, which in turn prepared the ground for his personal meeting with Sidi Abdelslam. This personal encounter, and his deep reading in the writings of Frithjof Schuon, brought Merton briefly to the exciting thought that through a special relationship with Schuon he might actually be able to insert himself into the genuine Sufi tradition, all the while deepening his own Christian commitment. But Merton came to see that authentic inter-religious dialogue meant not crossing the boundaries of his own faith commitment, even while gaining an ever deeper awareness and appreciation of Islam. His experience carries an important message for those of us who today strive to come to a deep understanding of Islam and a sense of interpersonal communion with Muslims in the search for peace and harmony in a world in which many people fear only a "clash of civilizations."[3]

One can only speculate about what Thomas Merton would make of the intrusion of a religiously warranted terror into Christian/Muslim relations in the late-twentieth century, a terror that in 1996 even consumed the lives of seven French Trappist monks, who, inspired by the teachings of Louis Massignon, were striving to live their monastic lives inter-religiously, in lived witness to their Christian faith, among the Muslims of Algeria.[4] The events of 9/11, the wars in Afganistan and Iraq, the renewed threat of nuclear war and mutual assured destruction that dominate our headlines today all evoke themes that engaged Merton in the sixties. Maybe that is why even forty years after his death there is scarcely a bookstore in the United States that does not stock several Merton titles even now. From the inter-religious perspective, his ideas are still fresh.

Thomas Merton never intended to develop an inter-religious or comparative theology from a Roman Catholic perspective. The focus of his concern was very much on his personal experience with those with whom he corresponded. Within this framework, almost intuitively, he nevertheless articulated thoughts that are striking for their immediate relevance to today's inter-religious encounters. For example, in his journal Merton spoke of meeting his correspondent "on a common ground of spiritual Truth, where we share a real and deep experience of God." He spoke of working toward a "conversion of us both," "upwards," "a real growth, an interior development."[5] And in a letter to Abdul Aziz, Merton spoke of "the sharing of the experience of the divine light, and first of all of the light that God gives us."[6] And while he called attention to the divisive potential of too much concentration on what he called "the realm of words and ideas,"[7] Merton was nevertheless sensitive to the importance of dogmatic statements and of the necessity to confess the truth they enshrine. Hence his reluctance, as we have seen, too readily to adopt the practices of other religious traditions uncritically or too easily to espouse the idea of the "transcendental unity of religions" as espoused by Frithjof Schuon.

Islam is a special case in that its spiritual exercises, especially as they are formulated in Sufism, bear an uncanny relationship to Christian ascetical and mystical principles. Thomas Merton very quickly resonated with them. But in its confessional dimension, Islam's teaching about the absolute "oneness" of God and the prophetic role of Muhammad is a direct critique of historical Christianity's confession of the doctrines of the Trinity, the Incarnation, and the saving event of Jesus the Christ's redemptive death on the cross. Merton did not offer any ideas about how Christians and Muslims might approach the discussion of these matters. Here there is a long history of mutual Christian/Muslim incomprehension, beginning already in the world of Islam[8] and compounding itself in the long polemical traditions of western Christianity.[9] But one thing is sure; he would have counseled us to begin with friendship. One imagines that Thomas Merton would be delighted with the open letter from 138 (and now more) Muslim leaders entitled, "A Common Word between Us and You," addressed on November 18, 2007 to a long list of world religious leaders, beginning with Pope Benedict XVI.[10] It seems that a new era of Christian/Muslim dialogue is in the offing, and for the conduct of this dialogue Thomas Merton still has much to teach us.

**Notes**

1. Merton, Thomas, *Mystics and Zen Masters* (New York: Farrar, Straus & Giroux, 1967).
2. Merton, Thomas, *The Way of Chuang-Tzu* (New York: New Directions, 1965).
3. See, e.g., the still very influential book by Samuel P. Huntington, *The Clash of Civilizations and the Remaking of World Order* (New York: Simon and Schuster, 1996).
4. See the gripping account by Kiser, John W., *The Monks of Tibhirine: Faith, Love, and Terror in Algeria* (New York: St. Martin's Press, 2002).
5. Merton, Thomas, *A Search for Solitude*, pp. 273-74.
6. Merton, Thomas, *The Hidden Ground of Love*, p. 54.
7. Merton, Thomas, *The Hidden Ground of Love*, p. 54.
8. See Griffith, Sidney H., *The Church in the Shadow of the Mosque: Christians and Muslims in the World of Islam* (Princeton, NJ: Princeton University Press, 2008).
9. See Armour, Rollin, *Islam, Christianity, and the West: A Troubled History* (Maryknoll, NY: Orbis Books, 2002).
10. See the text and numerous other related developments at the official website of the Muslim coordinating group: http://www.acommonword.com.

# WHAT TO LISTEN FOR
## Merton as Teacher—A Note

### Victor A. Kramer and Glenn Crider

Hundreds of hours of tape: a hundred hours commercially released; scores of lectures selected and reviewed,[1] yet we have hardly begun to listen. An aspect of Merton, barely heard, are the voice recordings made from his hundreds of hours of lectures, often given on Sunday afternoon for his community. They are full of insight, often topical, as when he speaks informally about the death of Martin Luther King, Jr.[2] An example of the value of Merton's taped lectures is seen within a large group devoted to an investigation of Cassian in relation to fundamental questions about prayer.[3]

### Notes

1. Published in *The Merton Annual: Studies in Culture, Spirituality & Social* Concerns, and indexed in Vol. 17, ed. Victor A. Kramer (Louisville, KY: Fons Vitae, 2004), p. 318: *The Merton Tapes*: Lectures by Thomas Merton. Review by Victor A. Kramer. 2 (1989), pp. 314-19; *The Merton Tapes* 2 [Second Series], Review by Dewey Weiss Kramer. 3 (1990), pp. 311-20; *The Merton Tapes* 3 [Third Series], Review by Victor A. Kramer. 5 (1992), pp. 362-68; *The Merton Tapes* 4 [Fourth Series], Review by Dewey Weiss Kramer. 6 (1993), p. 235; *The Merton Tapes* 5 [Fifth Series], Review by Steven L. Baumann. 7 (1994), pp. 176-78; *The Merton Tapes* 6 [Sixth Series], Review by Richard D. Parry. 9 (1996), pp. 264-66; *The Merton Tapes* 7 [Seventh Series], Review by David King. 12 (1999), pp. 235-39.
2. The following excerpt from Merton's taped lectures appears in *The Merton Annual: Studies in Culture, Spirituality & Social Concerns*, Vol. 16, ed. Victor A. Kramer (New York: Continuum, 2003), pp. 14-16. "First of all, the question of the death of Martin Luther King [Jr] is a little closer to home than you realize. You probably don't know the details. Some friends of his and of mine—mutual friends—in Atlanta were discussing with Martin Luther King about his coming here for a retreat in preparation for the march in Washington. And one of the times when he could have come was last week and they were sort of thinking about [this]

and I got this letter from this Quaker woman in Atlanta written on Wednesday which was the day that Martin Luther King went to Memphis. So I will just read what she says:

> Wednesday: Martin is going to Memphis today and I learned he won't be back until the weekend so John will see him next week. I was going to talk to him tomorrow and get another plan going. If the Memphis march becomes violent again there will be a terrible shattering for him. I hope both he and [Thich] Nhat Hanh will soon go to Gethsemani. (Nhat Hanh is this Buddhist from Viet Nam.) If Martin had taken a period there at Gethsemani he might have had the wisdom and repose to stay out of Memphis in the first place. And it was a mistake to go there. He had done no preparation and came in cold to a hot situation where the young militants had him just where they wanted him.

So, in other words, it was kind of a crucial and providential thing—he might have come here and if he had come here he would not have gone to Memphis, and if he had not gone to Memphis he would not have been killed. Of course, one of the things you need to understand is that this whole race situation is much more complicated right now than it looks to us because there's a big division within the [African Americans] themselves.

Most of the [African Americans] don't want this violence and they're trying to keep this thing non-violent and they're trying to keep it quiet. And you've got a lot of young kids who are very mad and very fanatical, and they're not really members—some are members of [a] certain movement—others aren't. And they are trying to push the violence. He was actually caught between those two groups in Memphis.

And that was what made it so tough for him. What he was trying to do was to keep the whole thing non-violent and keep it from erupting. And they were trying to push it into violence. They were trying to stimulate violence. So he was caught there. And it's a very complicated situation.

Now, another thing is too that you're liable to hear at the moment—you sort of get the impression that since this has happened the [African Americans] are blowing up all over the place. Well, yes and no. And they're not all mad either. Don't get that idea. But there is violence, of course, here and there. But just to give you a funny and strange example of how this works: today, quite by surprise, two young [Black] men and a White man came in [to the Abbey Guesthouse] from the Ghetto district of Cleveland. I got a message to come and see them. They said, 'Well, we're living the monastic life in Cleveland and we wanted to talk to you about it' and so forth and so forth. And now the first thing about this is that they came from this tough section of Cleveland and I said, 'Is there anything happening there?' They said no everything is alright.

All they wanted to talk about was this monastic life they started. They rented a house for 50 dollars a month. The place is falling down but anyway they can live in it. And there they have a nucleus of people living the monastic life—mostly centered on meditation. Well where they meditate is in the attic. They just get up in the attic and meditate. There is not much more than a bare roof. And, incidentally, I handle all kinds of monastic problems around here. Characteristic 'monastic problems' with these kids—you know what it is—what do you do when the neighbors come in and beat you up and tear the place up? You know, so this is the monastic life! But what they've got going spiritually is meditation. It cuts across all kinds of denominations."

3. By Kramer, Victor A. and published in *The Merton Annual: Studies in Culture, Spirituality & Social Concerns*, Vol. 2, ed. Robert E. Daggy *et al* (New York: AMS Press, 1989), pp. 318-19. "This group of eight tapes (AA2067 through AA2074) may prove to be the most interesting of the talks. This is an extended series of sixteen investigations. Each of the lectures is self-contained and any one could (as an example, for this review) be discussed at length. The first five tapes (10 lectures) set the stage for the one labeled 'Prayer and the Active Life' (AA2072). Each of these lectures builds on basic ideas of Cassian. Trials; faith; disposition; the 'Our Father' as a fundamental form of prayer; and God's hearing of our method of prayer are the subjects. Merton's job is to show how the development of a method of prayer is a long, slow, arduous process. In the lectures about Cassian which he has earlier established as basic building blocks: one does not become a contemplative easily; troubles, testing, trials are basic. Merton notes: 'The basis of the contemplative life is an active life which is rooted in humility and obedience.'

Merton's gift of pulling together what may appear to be disparate ideas is beautifully exhibited in the set of two lectures about how the active and contemplative lives complement each other. We have to learn to train ourselves *not* to look at ourselves as the center. How does Merton stress this? Usually by taking a basic idea and examining it carefully. He takes a basic text 'Behold the Bridegroom cometh ...' and then stresses our fundamental way of life (monks, all Christians) as exiles allows us to perceive the life of God incarnated in real existential situations.

Merton's method—raising questions; joking; circling back; telling anecdotes; and then stressing basic insights—shows that as teacher he knew how to give students enough, but not so much that they become lost. In one of these Cassian tapes he says, 'Vocation is not something that is filed away. Vocation is something that you work at by free response. You judge by the concrete facts. These facts are manifestations of what God has planned.' These lectures are often informal, but that is one of their positive values. Some listeners may wish that these talks had been edited and repetitions eliminated. They are, however, more effective in their uncut versions. Merton's students were a mixed group, some with college educations, and others with only high school educations. The beauty of these tapes is that they reveal Merton's gift of reaching a diverse audience. This review has implied the value of these lectures. Let me now be more specific. Merton as teacher accomplishes several things here:

1) He provides basic information.
2) He ties the spiritual life into fundamental psychological and historical patterns.
3) He ties all this together while avoiding making it dry or abstract."

# BOOK

**Thomas Merton**
*Cassian and the Fathers: Initiation into the Monastic Tradition*. **Edited with an Introduction by Patrick F. O'Connell. Foreword by Patrick Hart, OCSO. Preface by Columba Stewart, OSB. Monastic Wisdom Series 1** (Kalamazoo, Michigan: Cistercian Publications, 2005), pp. lxvi + 304. ISBN 978-0-87907-001-4 (paperback). $29.95.

**Thomas Merton**
*Pre-Benedictine Monasticism: Initiation into the Monastic Tradition 2*. **Edited with an Introduction by Patrick F. O'Connell. Preface by Sidney H. Griffith. Monastic Wisdom Series 9** (Kalamazoo, Michigan: Cistercian Publications, 2006), pp. lxix + 391. ISBN 978-0-87907-073-1 (paperback). $24.95.

**Thomas Merton**
*An Introduction to Christian Mysticism: Initiation into the Monastic Tradition 3*. **Edited with an Introduction by Patrick F. O'Connell. Preface by Lawrence C. Cunningham. Monastic Wisdom Series 13** (Kalamazoo, Michigan: Cistercian Publications, 2008), pp. lviii + 416. ISBN 978-0-87907-013-7 (paperback). $39.95.

These three Merton volumes are among the initial offerings of the new Monastic Wisdom Series published by Cistercian Publications. In each, Patrick F. O'Connell has expertly edited and annotated lecture notes prepared by Merton during his term as novice master at the Abbey of Gethsemani (1955-1965) for various courses on Christian monastic and mystical traditions. Premiere scholars of the subjects treated in each volume have written Prefaces that help the reader understand just how pioneering Merton's interests were for the late 1950s and early 1960s. O'Connell's ample Introductions explain the historical context of the lectures and discuss Merton's personal engagement with and indebtedness to the figures and traditions he is teaching. He often finds pertinent passages from Merton's letters and journals that demonstrate his reflections on the courses as they were being taught. O'Connell provides a survey of the topics treated in each course and offers synthetic remarks on Merton's approach and teaching. Each Introduction also describes the surviving witnesses to the texts of the lectures and in Appendix A of each volume O'Connell has supplied abundant textual notes. He is to be commended for his meticulous attention to detail in the editing of these texts.

Besides those interested in learning more about the monastic and mystical traditions treated by Merton, scholars and others interested more generally in his thought and personality will find in these books a hitherto largely inaccessible aspect of the man which complements and at times contrasts with the "public" Merton found in his works written for publication, the "interpersonal" Merton revealed in his letters, and the "intimate" Merton unveiled in his recently published journals. These works thus constitute a unique perspective for those engaged in the retrieval of Merton's ideas and in the reconstruction of his monastic and personal identity.

The breadth of the topics covered in these lectures reveals the scope of Merton's wide-ranging interests. In *Cassian and the Fathers*, O'Connell presents Merton's lecture notes for two courses given to novices on multiple occasions from around 1955 to 1962. The first course is called the "Prologue to Cassian" and consists of a review of ascetic and monastic spirituality from the apostolic fathers onward, with the emphasis on the fourth century. The second course is the "Lectures on Cassian." Here, Merton begins by summarizing Cassian's life and teaching and then examines key sections of both the *Institutes* and *Conferences*. A brief survey of the contents of these two courses follows.

The "Prologue to Cassian" is largely derived from others' scholarship, particularly in the earlier sections which summarize pre-fourth-century spirituality. There are four topics covered in these early sections: martyrdom and virginity in the first and second century, aberrant movements (Encratism, Montanism, Neoplatonism, and Gnosticism), Clement of Alexandria, and Origen. Once he turns to the monastic figures of the fourth century, Merton depends more on his own reading of the primary texts and secondary scholarship. He deals with Antony the Great, Pachomius, Basil of Caesarea, Gregory of Nazianzus, Gregory of Nyssa, Palestinian monasticism, including Jerome, Mesopotamian and Syrian monasticism, the desert fathers of Nitria and Scete and their apophthegmata, and Evagrius Ponticus. As a whole, these sections are better than the preceding as Merton's own greater engagement with these topics and thinkers is evident.

In "Lectures on Cassian," Merton relies more upon his own reading of Cassian. His narration of Cassian's life affords him the opportunity to summarize the contents of various *Conferences* as he tracks Cassian's progress through Egypt. His longer summaries are often filled with his own insight and observations and list the key points of the conference. Merton next turns to a brief account of the Origenist controversy, which precipitated Cassian's departure from Egypt. He then recounts Cassian's progress from Egypt to Constantinople and then to Marseilles, where he founded a monastery. This travelog gives Merton the opportunity to speak briefly of John Chrysostom, Martin of Tours, Lerinian monasticism, and Caesarius of Arles, all but the first important for situating Cassian's monastic project in Gaul. The narrative of Cassian's life completed, Merton next turns to a detailed survey of the *Institutes* and *Conferences* 1, 2, 4, 9, 10, and 16. These sections are astute distillations of Cassian's monastic doctrine. Furthermore, Merton continually tries to relate the monastic practices and teachings described by Cassian to the disciplines of his own monastery, modifying Cassian if necessary.

*Pre-Benedictine Monasticism* represents a renewed attempt on the part of Merton to introduce monastic novices to the riches of ancient monastic spirituality. These notes are the basis for two lecture series that Merton gave to a newly combined novitiate of lay brothers and choir monks from early 1963 until August 15, 1965, five days before leaving for the hermitage. Compared with *Cassian and the Fathers*, these lecture series are chronologically more focused and culturally more diverse. Merton limits himself to the fourth through sixth centuries, and his coverage of Syriac monasticism constitutes half of the course. In the following review of the subjects treated in these two courses, I will compare them to his previous discussion of the same in *Cassian and the Fathers*.

The first lecture series deals exclusively with Greek and Latin sources: Paulinus of Nola, Martin of Tours, Antony the Great, Rufinus, John Cassian, Pachomian monasticism, Basil of Caesarea, Roman monasticism in Palestine, and Egeria. The brief sketches of Paulinus of Nola and Martin of Tours focus more on their lives than their monastic doctrine. Unlike in *Cassian and the Fathers*, where Merton's treatment of Antony's doctrine depends solely on the *Life of Antony*, here Merton discusses Antony's apophthegmata as "the best, simplest, most authentic résumé of Antonian spirituality" (p. 20). Unfortunately, his treatment of these apophthegmata is a mere summary of their themes without much commentary. As for Rufinus, Merton focuses primarily on Rufinus's translation of the *Historia Monachorum*. His section on Cassian nicely complements his extensive treatment in *Cassian and the Fathers* because he had recently come across Salvatore Marsili's book that compared Evagrius of Pontus and Cassian. This results in a fresh treatment of some of the *Conferences* informed by Marsili's scholarship. Though Merton had discussed Pachomius and Pachomian monasticism in *Cassian and the Fathers*, his treatment here is far better. In his earlier treatment, Merton was limited to using Jerome's Latin translation of the Pachomian rules. Here, Merton avails himself of other primary texts and recent scholarship on Pachomius done by Louis Lefort and Heinrich Bacht. Merton next turns to Basil of Caesarea, whom he had treated briefly in *Cassian and the Fathers*. Merton's lengthier discussion here is far superior. He comments on a number of "Basilian" texts, all of which were viewed in antiquity as authored by Basil, but modern scholarship has judged that some of them are not by him. The next section, on Roman monasticism in Palestine, is more satisfying than a similar section in *Cassian and the Fathers*. He briefly describes the monasticism of Jerome and Paula at Bethlehem, and that of the two Melanias on the Mount of Olives, and then considers some texts. What comes next is without parallel in *Cassian and the Fathers*: an interesting discussion of the *Pilgrimage of Egeria*. Merton reviews the scholarship concerning the actual name of the author of this text (still a much-disputed question) and summarizes the biblical character of her spirituality, her understanding of pilgrimage, and her view of monks. He then runs through her descriptions of the monks she encounters.

The second lecture series focuses on Syriac monasticism. Merton's treatment of Mesopotamian and Syrian monasticism in *Cassian and the Fathers* was little more than a list of names. But Merton's reading of recent scholarship led him to re-evaluate the Syriac tradition. His discussion of Syriac monasticism begins with a review of Syriac Christianity: its influences, its origins, its early figures, movements, and literature. Next Merton deals with Theodoret, Aphrahat, Ephrem, Syrian monastic rules, and Philoxenus of Mabbug. In his treatments of Theodoret and Aphrahat, Merton, very dependent on others' scholarship, seems not to have thought too deeply about what he read, content to summarize rather than analyze. The same trend continues when Merton comes to discuss Ephrem, where he depends upon the scholarship of Edmund Beck and others. After a brief summary of Syrian monastic rules and their themes, Merton turns to Philoxenus of Mabbug. He begins by summarizing Philoxenus's life, works, homilies, and doctrine, drawing from Eugène Lemoine's introduction to his translation. Merton then discusses his homilies and letters, not sequentially but thematically. Here for the first time when discussing the Syriac material he really seems engaged by it. Merton is at his best when he discusses Philoxenus, showing himself analytical and insightful.

*An Introduction to Christian Mysticism* was not intended for nor presented to the novices. The course was given in 1961 to young priests for their ongoing formation in mystical theology. Merton describes the purpose of the course as "not to cover every detail and aspect of the subject, but to look over the whole field, to *coordinate* and *deepen* the ascetic knowledge that it is presumed everybody has, and to orient that asceticism to the mystical life" (p. 15; italics his emphasis). After introductory matters, the course covers the mystical theology of the Gospel of John, martyrdom as the summit of the mystical life, Christian gnosis, divinization in the Greek fathers (particularly the Cappadocians), Evagrius Ponticus, natural contemplation (particularly in Maximus the Confessor), the Dionysian tradition of mystical theology, Western mysticism (particularly Augustine and medieval Latin mysticism), fourteenth-century mysticism (the Beguines and Rhineland mystics), and Spanish mysticism (mainly Teresa of Avila). The course concludes with discussions of the spiritual direction of contemplatives and the relation between spiritual direction and psychotherapy. In his discussion of these figures and movements, Merton for the most part depends on secondary scholarship, not his personal reading. However, he rarely limits himself to one source (as was often the case in *Cassian and the Fathers* and *Pre-Benedictine Monasticism*).

Merton has read other scholars' work with care and attention, and he offers a critical assessment of contemporary viewpoints on the figures treated in the course. And so, these lecture notes reveals Merton at his synthetic and analytic best.

As these three books are published in Cistercian Publication's Monastic Wisdom Series, the following question should be asked, as suggested by the subtitles: are these books any good for initiating monastic novices or others into the monastic and mystical traditions? A detailed answer cannot be given here. But a few general observations can be made. Without a doubt, Merton was engaged with some of the best critical scholarship of his era, and his lectures reflect this. Nonetheless, in the light of more recent scholarship, his treatment of individual *figures* and *movements* is at times deficient and outdated (as one would expect). Despite this, his discussion of particular *texts* is on the whole very good. Merton was a careful and insightful reader of monastic and mystical literature, and had the rare ability to digest the main themes of any text and re-express them clearly, succinctly, and intelligently. His treatments of the many classic monastic and mystical texts that he discusses therefore remain valuable as good introductions to these texts. A reader of monastic and mystical literature would be well served by taking Merton as his or her initial guide through the texts he discusses, especially if it is complemented by reading more recent scholarship. For this purpose, O'Connell has supplied updated bibliographies for the subjects dealt with in each volume.

–Mark DelCogliano

# CONTRIBUTORS

**Glenn Crider**, production manager and editorial contributor for *The Merton Annual: Studies in Culture, and Social Concerns*, Vols. 14-20, served as co-chair of the Atlanta Chapter of The International Thomas Merton Society, 2001-2003. He holds the M.Div. and Th.M. in historical theology from Emory University.

**Kathleen Deignan**, CND, PhD, is a sister of the Congregation of Notre Dame and Professor of Religious Studies at Iona College where she directs the Iona Spirituality Institute. She is composer in residence with Schola Ministries, a project in service to the liturgical and contemplative arts which has produced a dozen CDs of her original sacred songs. Her recent books are *When the Trees Say Nothing: Thomas Merton's Writings on Nature*, and *Thomas Merton: A Book of Hours*. She is completing her GreenFaith Fellowship training for religious environmental leaders; http://www.KathleenDeignan.org.

**Mark DelCogliano** is a doctoral student in religion at Emory University, where he studies patristics. He has published articles on patristic theology and monastic topics, and book reviews and translations, in *Cistercian Studies Quarterly*, *The Benedictine Review*, *Cîteaux: Commentarii cistercienses*, *Journal of Early Christian Studies*, *Journal of Theological Studies*, *Orientalia Christiana Periodica*, and *Zeitschrift für Antikes Christentum*.

**Victor A. Kramer**, emeritus professor of English, Georgia State University, is a founding member of The International Thomas Merton Society; founding editor of *The Merton Annual: Studies in Culture, Spirituality, and Social Concerns*, and editor of Merton's complete journal, Vol. 4, *Turning Toward the World: The Pivotal Years, 1960-1963*. His book *Thomas Merton, Monk and Artist* was published by Cistercian Publications. He is a Certified Spiritual Director and teacher for Spring Hill College in Atlanta.

**Patrick F. O'Connell**, associate professor of English and Theology at Gannon University, Erie, PA, is a founding member and former president of the International Thomas Merton Society and edits the ITMS quarterly, *The Merton Seasonal*. He is coauthor of *The Thomas Merton Encyclopedia* (2002) and editor of *The Vision of Thomas Merton* (2003) and of four volumes of Merton's monastic conferences: *Cassian and the Fathers* (2005), *Pre-Benedictine Monasticism* (2006), *An Introduction to Christian Mysticism* (2008) and *The Rule of St. Benedict* (2009).

**Malgorzata Poks** holds a doctorate in American Literature from the University of Lublin, Poland. Her interests concern spirituality and modern American poetry, especially the poetry of Thomas Merton and Denise Levertov. She teaches at the English Teacher Training College in Sosnowiec, Poland.

www.ingramcontent.com/pod-product-compliance
Lightning Source LLC
Chambersburg PA
CBHW040300170426
43193CB00020B/2960